The SAMUEL SHOEMAKER Library

REVIVE

THY CHURCH

BEGINNING

WITH ME

By

SAMUEL M. SHOEMAKER

WORD BOOKS
PUBLISHER
WACO, TEXAS

Table of Contents

"The name of Cheng Ching-yi is indelibly associated with the slogan 'Lord, revive thy church, beginning with me,' which he gave to the Chinese Forward Movement of Evangelism in 1928. . . . As one of the youngest delegates at the Edinburgh Conference in 1910 he made fame for himself by a seven-minute speech in which he educed seven reasons for recognizing the maturity of the Chinese church as a partner in the world enterprise and a companion in world evangelization."

From the book *Committed Unto Us* by WILLIS LAMOTT, p. 151

Preface

There are three kinds of books about religion: "why" books, "what" books, and "how" books. The "why" books deal with the reasons for being Christians at all. The "what" books deal with the content of the Christian message. And the "how" books deal with practical ways of making religion real and workable for oneself and for other people. The writer would like this book to be a small contribution to the "how" literature of contemporaneous Christianity.

There are many "how" books about the spiritual life, and they are badly needed. Such books may have two limitations: (1) they may seem to ignore the "what" and the "why" of religion, whereas the "how" has no significance except in conjunction with them; and (2) they may appear to assume in their authors some special spiritual insight, or "human" understanding, which is probably more the authors' aspiration than their possession. But books on the "how" of religion should at least avoid the temptation of some writings on the "why" and the "what" to flee from life's immediacies and practicalities, by retreating into the upper ether of religious theory.

There is not time, in a book like this, to go into many of the basic questions of religion. One would better read William Temple's *Christ the Truth*, or J. S. Whale's *Christian Doctrine*, or the fine summary of the Gospel in *Towards the Conversion of England*, pages 11 to 35. The aim of this book is to make our faith, which is the greatest possession we have, more potent in our lives, and to enable us to commend it more effectually to others.

A clergyman writes: "*How* are we to evangelize? *How* are we to start serious conversations that will deepen the spiritual lives of our people in our parish calling? How do we make an approach to the non-Christian? Do we wait until they approach us? ——— has a little book out on winning people to the Church, but little about the more important job of winning them to Christ." Such questions as these are in the minds of many. I have not set out to answer each of them, though I hope that some indication of answers will be found in what I have said. One can at best only indicate suggestions of the "how" of dealing with people. The actual doing of it is inseparable from the nature and temperament of the person who seeks to do it, and comes out of him in ways distinctive to himself. It is rather a flavor, an atmosphere, the suggestion of some universal principles, and the dynamic of experience which one can bring to another in these matters. Too much rule-of-thumb and one-two-three would not channel but stifle the Spirit one wants to release.

It is perhaps inevitable that a book which comes up out of one's deepest convictions, and the experience that lies closest to one's own heart, should be rather personal. "We speak that we do know, and testify that we have seen." Such a sentence must begin in the first person. But one hopes that this does not create the impression, either that one "has all the answers," or that one is presenting an infallible panacea or nostrum. Naturally one writes of ways and means that have proven useful. But the human spirit is so varied, God's ways with us so mysterious, and our own role as would-be bridge between the two so often blocked by our own frailties, that one becomes very much aware that other persons and procedures may be more effective, and that all of us fail sometimes, often tragically. Even when one has insight, understands people, and knows something of "the ways of God" with man, he often fails to apply what he knows. Yet the things I have put down in this book have had a fairly wide testing, and are the fruit of the experience of many others beside myself. It is this which makes me think they may have a general application and validity.

It looks as though our world, in the next twenty-five years, would go either way up, or way down. Which way depends, frankly and almost totally, upon whether we can so put ourselves at God's disposal that He can bring to the world, through people like ourselves, the thing which it needs most. We cannot doubt either His power, or his willingness: any blockage must be on our side. If all of us will try to get the ways open to Him, and become His agents and His instruments, we may make possible that flooding down of God's free and plentiful Grace which is, among all our human needs, the sorest need of our time and of our world.

S. M. S.

Revive Thy Church
Beginning with Me

CHAPTER I

The Need and Our Resources

THERE is a general feeling in the hearts of average men, borne out by facts known to the experts, that our world is at a parting of the ways. We are about to take a course that will lead upwards into a new age, or one that will lead downwards into nihilism. The crisis of our time is wholly unprecedented. Civilization is going round a corner on two wheels. Whether it will right itself, or skid off into disaster, is the still unanswered question. The world has faced crises before now, but this one seems to concern all mankind at one time. Above it all hangs the threat of the destructive power of the split atom, augmented by the allegedly even more dangerous threat of a germ-war that can be released at any time. We all tremble from the effects of the situation. Only the most blind or unfeeling are exempt from an undercurrent of anxiety about the future, as if mankind might be living on borrowed time. Men seem to have an emotion not dissimilar to that of animals as they approach the stockyard: things have an ominous smell. As Dr. Elton Trueblood says, "Millions are fatalistic. They feel utterly powerless in the presence of forces which they can neither understand nor control. In spite of our proud achievements . . . there is a wide-spread sense that we are waiting for a catastrophe."

We might as well look the black facts squarely in the face. Dr. Robert M. Hutchins, Chancellor of the University of Chicago, says that the United States has stockpiled enough atom bombs to wipe out every major city in the world, and has enough reserves of bacterial missiles to kill every person the bombs did not kill. He says, "We have at most three years to forestall annihilation."

Not alone in the field of science, but in the political field as well, we face the gravest dangers. The forces which work for the overthrow of those conditions which foster free institutions get in their licks every hour. Felix Morley tells us concerning our own country that "administrative law, already dangerously developed, could with little change become government by outright decree. The Federal structure . . . would in fact if not in name be supplanted by strongly centralized authority in every field of social activity. The one-party system, now advocated in effect by many who are not consciously fellow travellers, might take permanent root. The United States could easily become a single authoritarian, totalitarian State." And concerning England, Dr. C. K. Allen, Professor of Jurisprudence at Oxford, says, "Does the ordinary citizen realize that he is being steadily stripped of the defenses which for centuries have stood between him and autocracy?"

The public crisis is, as always, mirrored in the personal crisis, where perhaps its only final solution must also be found. Let two illustrations suffice. There are in the United States 182 state institutions for the mentally sick, with 560,000 patients in them: one out of every twenty persons born in this country will spend part of his life in these institutions. There are 750,000 chronic alcoholics in this country, many of them women; and there are two or three million excessive drinkers from whom the chronic alcoholics are recruited. We must all realize that there is something of escapism in much mental sickness and alcoholism. Both are symptomatic of a time when many have lost their grip on life and do not know how to regain it. The proportion of self-reliant, ambitious, well-adjusted people is certainly less in our society, and we see everywhere about us nerveless, dependent and poorly adjusted individuals. If this be true in the most favored nation on earth, what must be taking place elsewhere? With so much of defeat and disgust with ourselves running through our own lives and emotions, it is no wonder if we feel a foreboding that someone will arise who will express the gathered subconscious fears, resentments and despairs of the race, as Hitler did those of the German people after World War I, and blow us to pieces. Our world is sick without and sick within. There is a tragic powerlessness even in men of faith and good will, even in all of them taken together, to do much about it. With no power to draw together even the broken fragments of our homes and our personal lives, what can we say to heal the scattered and desperate fragments of mankind?

We need help, and we need it quickly. We need hope and faith, for without them we can only wring our hands. Help can hardly come from something new that might be brought on the scene to ease the crisis. There simply is not time for that, even if such a force were anywhere manifest, as it is not. Is there anything here, already known, already having some traction and headway? Our thoughts turn to our traditional Christianity in a flash of hope. This may change quickly to misgiving. For the power of Christianity seems to have got grounded somehow

The Church seems as hopelessly implicated in the modern mess as all the rest of mankind—as much party to things as they are, as little inspired with the timely word or plan. Can the creaking wheels of the Church's machinery be oiled by some new spirit, so that they begin turning fast enough to meet today's demand for a new output of inspired personalities, and to bring the spiritual answer for mankind?

Harold Laski says that Christianity can provide an inspiring faith no longer. Are we to accept this judgment? Are we to remember from what kind of source it comes, and discount it? Dr. Elton Trueblood answers him that Christianity is true, not merely useful, and that what is true at any time is true always, and also that Christianity has a remarkable vitality and ability to "revive itself from within by unflinching self-criticism."

Let us consider six other viewpoints of men who believe that it is to Christianity that we must look for help and hope. They come from a poet, a military man, a philosopher, a historian and two scientists. T. S. Eliot says that society "so far as it is civilized is still Christian." General MacArthur says that "the problem basically is theological and involves a spiritual recrudescence and improvement of human character that will synchronize with our almost matchless advance in science, art, literature and all the material and cultural developments of the past 2000 years." Dr. William Ernest Hocking says that "it is only religion which, finding the ultimate solitude of the soul . . . can create the unpurchasable man. And it is only the man unpurchasable by any society that can create a sound society." Professor William Aylott Orton writes, "Liberalism . . . with Aristotle for its godfather, stands firm rooted in the Christian ethos: the only one that takes the human being in all his concrete imperfection, and with everlasting forbearance seeks to make the best of him. It is significant that liberalism and Christianity (of which it is the political application) in modern times went down together; and are now coming up together. . . . It is only in the Christian doctrine of man that we can find a firm and reasoned ground for (the) American affirmation." Dr. Lecomte du Noüy says, "[Man] needs enlightenment, encouragement, advice, consolation and hope. Efficient, disinterested help can only come to him from the wise, inspired human traditions represented by the Christian religion, heir to all the spiritual treasures of mankind and keeper of the eternal flame which the greatest and purest men have passed on to one another, from time immemorial, over the bodies of dying civilizations." And Dr. Arthur H. Compton says, "Recently there has been much talk to the effect that our knowledge and power are expanding faster than our moral sense. I do not believe it. Everything in our present world seems to belie the statement. Rather, I believe that the Creator of our universe has, from the beginning, had a plan for shifting moral responsibility on to man's shoulders as fast as he can take it. The mechanism of the shift is the increase of knowledge. That is the great propulsive force that pushes man inevitably to new heights and new strengths. The purpose is not to make man happy, but to make him great. With the raising of the curtain on the atomic age we have been called to unprecedented spiritual greatness."

Declarations like these are not soporific pills, to cause us to turn over and sleep on in our selfishness and blindness: they are challenges to you and to me personally to dig again the old wells of Christian faith, and bring up from them once more living water to cleanse and revive our world. The water is still there.

There seems to be none anywhere else. Christianity, with all its emphasis on the need for human change and transformation, turns out to be the one thing that stands permanently *on the side of man himself.* Our long-range self-interest lies in our present drastic self-criticism.

The most urgent question that we face is: What can bring faith back to the great mass of mankind? We should normally look to the churches for the new supply of needed faith, expecting those who already know its blessings to be the first to want to share them with others. Can the churches measure up? There are plenty of Christians on the rolls to change the face of the earth if they once got on fire about it. The world has more than six hundred million Christians in it: about 338,000,000 Roman Catholics, about 135,000,000 Protestants, and about 127,000,000 Orthodox. We have nearly 72,500,000 church members in America, and their numbers increased 32.8 per cent between 1926 and 1944. When you think what tiny minorities have done in countries like Russia and Germany within the past thirty years, and in the wrong direction, what might not this mighty force already existent begin to do, if the fire of the Spirit fell on it, and set it alight again as men were set alight at Pentecost? It is by no means impossible that a great awakening should take place in the churches, and spread to the nations and the world. Dr. K. S. Latourette, who has made the most exhaustive study of the history of Christianity in our time, thinks that the signs point to another spreading wave of awakening: he says, "More than at any time since the third century, the Christians of the world are drawing together. In this, the Holy Spirit is clearly at work. We are living in one of the great days of the Christian Church." And Dr. L. W.

Grensted, of Oxford, says, "I am sure that a religious revival is on its way. I am rather inclined to think that it has already begun. . . . I do not think that [it] will come with loud noise and under any obvious or outstanding leadership. It is more likely to be a broad and largely silent uprising, from the deeps of man's common spiritual heritage. It will reveal itself first, for those who have eyes to see, in little groups of people, often of widely different traditions, who have begun to find in fellowship an enriching of their spiritual life, and its power will lie in that deepening and enrichment, rather than in outward consequences, though consequences will follow, beyond our calculating or dreaming. I do not think that, as has happened before in history, it will be a movement of withdrawal from the world, but a movement by which our common everyday life . . . is laid bare to God's action and brought to its full meaning. And it will be world-wide."

When we say "the Church," we may be talking about one of two different churches. There is the truly converted Church—the Church that caught the fire of Christ's spirit and passed it on to future generations, the Church that kept that fire burning though often banked through the Dark Ages, the Church that produced St. Francis, the Church that (as Dr. Einstein said) alone "stood squarely across the path of Hitler's campaign for suppressing truth," the Church that the Reformation scholar Theodore Beza described to the King of Navarre as "an anvil that has worn out many hammers," the Church that is the Body and Bride of Christ, His creation and His love. All of us have at some time seen evidences of that Church, and been blessed by them. But then there is the unconverted Church—the Church that early lost its way in its relations to this world, became more concerned with means and methods than with objectives, the Church that persecuted those who dissented, the Church that drew its skirts about it in self-righteous exclusiveness, the load of hangers-on who are in the Church but not of it, who keep holding it back from its destiny because of the lazy unconvertedness of their own hearts, the Church that cannot effectively get out into the world and change it, because the world has already too effectively got into the Church and changed it instead.

Judgment must begin at the House of God. We cannot go through the world winnowing between chaff and wheat, separating between sheep and goats, parting men from their sins by calling them into new life, unless first we apply the process drastically to ourselves. If the Church of our day is to bring again to the world the faith and answer that it needs, something tremendous has got to happen to the Church as we know it. Karl Barth says, ". . . the true function of the Church consists first of all in its own regeneration. . . ." In this he takes up contemporaneously the ageless challenge which the great Danish master, Kierkegaard, gave to the Church a hundred years ago: "Christendom has done away with Christianity, without being quite aware of it. The consequence is that, if anything is to be done about it, one must try again to introduce Christianity into Christendom." Every word of that sentence tells. The fact is, we have lost what once we had: the early Church had it, ours has not. We are not quite conscious of it, not wishing to face so drastic a need, and being already inured to a comfortable, conventional brand of religion which we take to be the real thing. And, the place to start is with the reintroduction of Christianity into Christendom—that is, the reconversion of the Church to Jesus, and the renewal by His Holy Spirit of the kind of power it had in the early days, and has had from time to time since, when His winds blew once more upon its embers and fanned them into flame.

If it is to happen, it should happen in the obvious place where men go for religious help: *in our parishes.* There men and women should find the inspiration to transform the homes where they live, and the institutions in which they work. The change will come, not through different or even better parish organizations, not through new nostrums sent out by the church headquarters, and not alone through the importation of "new blood" in the shape of a visiting missioner or evangelist: it will come when ministers and laymen alike admit three things: (1) that the Church is not bringing to the desperate and open world of this time the answer of Jesus Christ, (2) that we are ourselves typical of the Church, and as such, responsible for its being what it is, and (3) that the change has got to begin in us and with us, before we can expect it to affect others, our parish, or our world.

How does this happen? There is a layman who has been senior warden of his parish. He is a public-spirited citizen, alert, interested in community welfare, and in maintaining the institution of the Church, giving generously to it. He has been going to church all his life. Yet nothing had ever in all those years been able to break through to the deepest desires of his heart. This caused a conflict in his life, from which he sought escape in alcohol, not habitually and to the point of chronic alcoholism, but so that it had a hold on him which he was not able to break. No one had ever made the religion of his Church so personal to him that he took action. He had no idea how to

cause his own faith to have any relevance for other men, nor
was he able to transmit this spirit to the large company of
which he has been for many years a senior officer. There are
tens of thousands of church members like him. They are the
backbone, and the despair, of every parish situation. Without
them we cannot function, yet with them we cannot function as
we should. What will bring the change?

We must get them in touch with the original fire somehow.
It may come through an honest talk with the minister, and
prayer together. With this man it came in one of the "little
groups" that Dr. Grensted mentions. It was a weekly meeting
mostly of laymen, who gather to talk about what God is doing
for them and with them, especially as regards the changing of
human relations in the business—that is usually the door by
which God comes into a business. The gathering was informal,
there was no pressure, there was much laughter, many took
part. The talk seemed to indicate an answer to the ordinary
problems of a business man's life and work. He felt a quiet
power there that he had never felt anywhere else. He went
several times, then he sought out the leader and had several
talks with him. Slowly the light dawned: he had never made
an unconditional surrender of himself to Jesus Christ. What
good was church work? What use in being another pew sitter?
What substitute were gifts of money? What God wanted was
his heart—his whole heart undivided. There came an hour
when he was absolutely honest with his friend. The crisis of
honesty is the beginning of the new life. When the backed-up
sins and compromises come clear out into the open, God can
get into the heart. He made his decision. Alcohol stopped almost
totally, though sometimes it is still a struggle. The great thing

was a complete change in outlook. His friends saw and re-
marked it. Shyly at first, but with increasing confidence, he
has been telling his friends what has happened to him—sending
them written material that will bear on their interests and
situations, watching for their responses and reactions. This
man who once merely helped to maintain an institution is now
out on the high seas of spiritual discovery and adventuring. He
spends an hour alone with God before he begins his working
day, and prayer is a living force in his life. We shall tell later
what is happening in his business as a result of his personal
experience.

Nine out of ten people who pick up this book will want to
go quickly past this initial step, and see what "plans" it offers,
what we must "do" in order to bring about a spiritual awakening in individuals, parishes, communities. They miss the point.
Until something happens *to* us and *in* us, it will not happen
through us. You could have put that man on a hundred committees, picked his good business brains for fine ideas—that was
what had been happening for forty years. We repeat piously
the little prayer, "O God, revive the Church, beginning with
me." Then we want to talk plans! The plans will be froth and
a waste of time unless the people who expect to carry them
out are first transformed by the Lord, examine their lives with
costly honesty, let go of all conscious compromise, and surrender
themselves to Him fully and finally. One of the things that is
making for discouragement in the Church today is the still-
born fruits of thousands of "plans" that fail because they do
not start with the planner. In twenty-five years, most of our
great communions have set out on from one to five different
ventures to produce spiritual awakening. They were mostly

determined to work with what they already had, hence the failure. If we stay as we are, we shall go on producing what we have produced. If we will let the Holy Spirit bring conviction of sin to us, and begin the completion of our own conversion, our plans will have life in them.

The great question, then, is: Shall we remain content with our present spiritual powerlessness, which (writ large) means the spiritual powerlessness of the Church; or shall we let a divine discontent come into our hearts, shall we pray and wrestle till we are blessed and changed, shall we ask God to take us over completely, and in spite of all our known weakness and inexperience to use us in human lives and situations? He has the power to give us if we will take it. Shall we ask for it—and take the consequences?

CHAPTER II

How People Find God

H OW does the spiritual experience take place? That is what we want to know. We put out endless books on the theory of religion, and its theology; and at times we need such source books. But what the average man wants to know is: *how*. How do people come by the transforming experience of God which makes life a new thing for them? Why do others miss it? Let us come now to grips with this.

The normal way to begin a religious experience is to be *brought up in a religious atmosphere*. It doesn't have to start that way, and many find it who did not find it in childhood. But that is the normal time. And the normal way is through a family that believes in religion, and a church to which the family goes together. Family prayers, some read, some spoken from the heart, with some Bible reading, and a little chance to talk over the day's plans in the light of them—these give children a foundation. Going to church Sunday after Sunday exposes a child in his most impressionable time to certain ideas and ideals that are characteristic of Christianity. It is all taken as a matter of course, and should be. There is always a chance that this early religion may seem so dull and stodgy that the child will later react from the false parts of it: he cannot react from the true parts without some violence to himself, for

Christianity is the revelation of what life is meant to be; he may have to go through some hard times to learn this, but his early training will stand him in good stead. It will stand there challenging him from within until he comes to terms with it. For those whose vital spiritual experience comes later in life, this early training constitutes nevertheless an invaluable help. So we find God, in the simplest way, by tradition.

We also find Him through *need*. The strains of adolescence, of a broken family, of difficult adjustments with schoolmates, may bring about this sense of need in youth. It may not come till much later in life. The longer one lives, the more he finds that life itself is the great evangelizer. Life seems so constituted that within it are to be found the very problems and needs that set us to thinking about God, wondering first, then seeking. Fulfillment and disillusionment are strangely mixed in our experience. Joy may drive us to God in sheer necessity for somebody to thank—sadness may drive us to Him in sheer necessity for somebody whom we can tell all about it. Inner defeat may so divide us and make us miserable that we seek the unification of ourselves in a discovery of God. Some persons will never find God till they experience a great sense of need. The kind of need that results in unhappiness is likely to be felt by the person himself; the kind of need that results, say, in wrong relations, or in unconscious hurting of others, may have to be recognized through some challenge from without. Perhaps the greatest need of all is the questions which life flings at us, demanding an answer: "What are you doing here?" "Where did you come from?" "Where are you going when you die?" We coast along easily for years—then death strikes suddenly and tragically by our side, and we have nothing with which to meet it. We consider our conventional religion satisfactory to ourselves—but one of the children turns to alcohol, another is divorced, and we see that our kind of religion is not sufficient for this person whom we love. This drives us deeper and makes us search for something more than we have had before. We look for God, for more of God, from a sense of *need*.

This sense of need may be provoked, however, by *exposure* to the faith of other people. They may be discovering things through religion, having experiences of its power to transform situations, that we are stranger to. One man says, "I was quite satisfied with routine church services and church work until I went to Northfield in the great days when John R. Mott and Robert E. Speer and others like them were speaking to hundreds of us school-boys and undergraduates: I never knew till then that Christianity was a mighty world-wide force that changed the lives of men. They awakened a hunger in me that had not been there before, as they did in tens of thousands more." Perhaps every person ought to supplement what he gets in his own church by some exposure to other groups than his own, ecumenical groups where he sees a different quality, special companies where inspiration comes from great leaders and speakers and from fellowship on a high level. We grow conventional and satisfied and dead when we chew our own cud too long.

The search may be instigated by a *book*. Writing which has spiritual fire in it can set hearts alight even with no personal contact. I know a man who once read a book while he was on a railroad journey, and it changed the rest of his life! One seeks to put down in a book what is general and universal and for everybody, and as people "see" themselves in books, they are carried along with the writer. Dr. E. Stanley Jones' book *Abundant Living* has been a perfect mine to those who are spiritually seeking. Agnes Sanford's book *The Healing Light* is opening up new vistas of faith and prayer in relation to health. Dr. Frank C. Laubach's *Prayer the Mightiest Force in the World* reveals the power behind his marvelously creative life of service. Melvin Evans' *It Works* will convince any business-man that he is missing something if he does not try to get his religion right into his business. We ought to have a shelf of books ready to lend people, and be careful to give them the right one at the right time.

People are often much more moved than we imagine by *preaching*. There is usually a strong element of teaching in our modern preaching, for people are spiritually illiterate these days; and preaching must have in mind the balance of the Christian message. But all preaching today should be funda-mentally evangelistic in intent, because as Dr. Visser 't Hooft says, we "preach to the world as if it were the Church"—as yet much of it is not, and must be won and converted before it is ready to be instructed. When a man's heart is warmed by God, and what he says comes through a trained mind, and an address which is thoroughly prepared, people are moved and stirred. Probably if we could examine the file cases down in our human subconscious we should find that there are very few sermons which have not left some deposit in our memories and which have not made some impression upon us. Often people have not heard the most obvious truths of Christianity, or failed to take them in; and when first they grasp one of those truths, something happens. I shall never forget as rather a small boy hearing the minister in our parish at home preaching about "Thy will be done"; he made it clear to us that this was not a matter of resignation but of co-operation, and was not meant to be carved on tombstones but on the hearts and wills of people. People are tired of religious essays musty with book learning but empty of contemporary life; they want the Gospel. Henry R. Luce, the editor of *Life* and *Time,* says: "We are thirsty for the truth! But we will be bored by stale moralisms or inept attempts to comment on current events. Do you know about God? That's what we, in the church and out of it, want to know." You can tell when a man has thought his way through the deeper problems of the faith, and when he is groping; you can also tell when he is spinning out ideas about religion, and when he is communicating to others a living faith. Preaching deals too much with the *why* and the *what*; it should deal much more with the *how.*

And some find God through the *personal witness* of others. Talk alone may be impertinent and ineffective; there must be something in one's life that challenges and satisfies the other person, gives him a new idea, puts a nick in his mind. Courageous living through tragedy, patience under pain, gentleness toward trying personalities, moral courage in face of wrong—such things open the door for witness. They become an "example," not in the priggish, prunes-and-prisms sense, but as living with an edge to it. This makes people curious, they may want to ask "how you get that way." One has to put his truth cogently and appropriately. One may say to a pagan, with a wink and a smile, "I like to talk things over with the Big Boss," and he will get what is meant; from there on out it is possible to talk freely about prayer, God, Jesus Christ, in a natural way,

not as an attitude, nor a tradition, nor a point of view, but as
power coming into daily living. Get on board with a pagan—
where he is—and he will be much more inclined to get on
board with you and your faith. We need a lot of play and
humor and naturalness in all this: many a gulf is bridged by
some laughter. But any man for whom faith is a reality can
make faith real to other people if he will talk about its effects
in a simple, natural, human way. Faith is very attractive, and
very contagious.

Sometimes it is a good thing to take people to a place *where
faith is at work*. A church service may be the right place, if
one can expect vital devotion and preaching, and some friendliness afterwards. A rescue mission where down-and-outs get
converted may mark the turning point for someone who has
considered himself "above" that kind of thing, till the Holy
Spirit shows him in the meeting that he, too, is down-and-out
inside, and needs the same tremendous redemption. A man
who had been for years a hard-drinking pagan went to a meeting
where other men talked quietly but enthusiastically about how
different life was when you trust God: there was evident a
"before" and "after" quality which sharpened for him the
sense that a religious experience was definite and available to
him. He had been to church services more than once, but no
one seemed to expect very much to happen. Here he saw men
in whom the Spirit of God was manifestly at work. If God
could come to them, He could come to him. A spark flew and
caught in his imagination which set alight a fire of faith which
has burned brightly for upwards of fifteen years. A minister
had been visiting another parish where real miracles in people's
lives take place, and on returning home was telling some of his

boys about his visit: one of them said to him, "Gee, is that what religion does? Why don't people get converted in our church?" Why don't they?

Thus far we have been speaking of the things which arouse curiosity, touch the imagination, and awaken a desire for faith. This must come first. To move on to next steps before this initial interest has been aroused is to court failure. If people come along with you then, it will be simply to become conventional religionists; more often it will turn them against the whole thing, and they will avoid religion and religious people thereafter. Henry Drummond said that the faculty of the new evangelism was the *imagination*. Until this has been touched and stirred, there is no use moving in on the mind or the will.

A minister wrote to a fellow clergyman, saying, "For years I have been plagued by tensions, nervous and muscular. My war experience accentuated them. How shall they be broken, and show shall I attain that 'peace that passeth understanding' against which they war? A psychiatrist is not the answer for I myself know their source: a lifetime of self-concern. Now that I am delivered into the power of the gospel, the vestiges of yesterday are not ready to depart. How shall these demons be cast out? There may be some area in which I am not surrendered, but I am not aware of it. I sense the problem to be one of breaking the evil habits which date back to childhood fears and emotional stresses over which I had no control." He was asked to come for a talk. A large, handsome, healthy-looking man, he has an alert, better-than-average mind; he is happily married and is the father of attractive children. His is a good, substantial church but he has always been consumed with a desire for a better one—"the distant fields are greener."

Thus he has felt like a squirrel in a cage, going round and round with movement but without direction. He readily responded to questions raised by his friend. Yes, his relations with his wife were happy and healthy. True, he did not give quite enough time to his children, and was apt to be "busy" whenever they wanted to be with him. His sermons were book-born, not life-born—they came out of solitary thinking and reading in his study, not out of the meeting of personalities in a living interview. Not much happened in his parish calls. People were helped, but not changed, in his church. He had a persistently negative approach, expecting failure. What to do?

He was like a well-arranged electrical system in a house, with the power not turned on. The problem was getting into real touch with God. His counselor suggested that God is more eager to get in touch with us than we to get in touch with Him, and if we would drop strain and effort, it might give Him a chance. As they talked he became quiet, very relaxed. He was told to release every tension in his body, let his arms go limp on the arms of the chair, his feet stretched out in front of him, and to pray for himself, as he was being prayed for. Ruminatively, quietly, slowly, this prayer began. It gave their whole minds to God. Everything—confession, petition, thanksgiving, spreading out their needs. There were enough interstices in that prayer for the Spirit to come in through it, to lift it, to use it for Himself. They were utterly natural, with no self-consciousness, lost in God and in prayer. Soon he took it up and prayed in the same way. He gave over to God his fears, his negative ways of thinking, his ambition, his tensions. It was a living experience of prayer, giving him a glimpse of a new world of the Spirit in which he had never lived before. They spoke of renewing this experience again and again privately. Later he wrote of "my ecstatic experience in your study" (it seemed quiet and unemotional enough when it took place), saying, "The tenseness of which I complained when I was with you has passed away in answer to our prayers. There is, moreover, a very positive note implanted in my heart. When I am in a tight spot and ask the Lord if He is with me, I get an answer which usually says this: 'Of course I'm with you.' I've a long way to go in my spiritual development—old ambitions still plague me—but the poison is pretty well pumped out. . . . We leave August 1 for vacation—when we return, I expect to launch one of the most intensive 'new life' crusades this parish has ever seen." He is ready for that now. Before, it would have been a thing of committees, gatherings, money, plans, but not of power. Now it can come *through* him, because first it happened *to* him.

Clearly, such a man had a well-defined need and wanted help. What about those who are not seeking? Well, any road may lead to Rome. Begin with people as they are. There is always a need, always a place to take hold. As Dr. Harry Emerson Fosdick says, a man is like an island; you have to row all around him to find a place to land. A young fellow went to call on a minister with his best-beloved: they wanted to be married. She was a church girl; he had been brought up in the church but said at the outset he was there only to be married—he had no interest in God or religion or the church. The minister knew that the uppermost thing in his mind was to make this the greatest marriage ever. What had faith to do with that? Could he relate it to what already interested this man. He told them about a similar couple who had come in to be married, and who had never talked over the question of religion together: she, too, was a Christian girl, but he was an intellectual skeptic, and she was afraid if she raised the question with him, he would quash her faith—so they left it untouched. The minister asked the young man how much basis for mutual understanding he thought there was in such an outlook; and he replied, "Not much." This opened the way to say that marriage needs a spiritual foundation. The parson talked a little about his own home, and others where God is a living factor. He asked the skeptical young man if he would be willing to consider the matter with an open mind, and he said he would. He gave him a pamphlet entitled *How to Find God,* and the book *Abundant Living.* A month later, a week before his wedding, the minister saw him again. He asked how he was getting along, and he replied, "Well, I am this far along—if I go to bed without saying my prayers, I don't sleep so well. . . . But where does Jesus Christ come into all this?" The minister picked up from his desk a card, much used during the war, with the head of Christ on one side, and the little biography of Him called "One Solitary Life" on the other, and handed it to his friend. He read it. "That's it," he said, "that's the missing piece in the puzzle."

Then the minister said to him that the question now was, what was he going to do about Jesus Christ—would he surrender his life to Him unconditionally and fully? Going on, he pointed out that this often means four things: (1) the readiness to be done with sin in every known form, (2) the willingness to pray and keep in touch with God daily, (3) the search for God's will in the investment of one's life—vocation, and marriage, and (4) the determination to win others to the Christian life. They took these up one by one, and in detail. The man was honest about his sins—temper, selfishness, the desire to have his own way. He wanted Christ now, and was devastatingly honest with himself and with his counselor. When it was all out (not before), the minister suggested they get on their knees and he make his decision. He had never prayed aloud with anyone before, but all that was lost in his intense desire to find and to have Christ. He poured out his very soul in honest confession; one terrific thing that had happened during the war came out through his prayer, and God's forgiveness of that was what really changed his life. He got up a new person, his eyes shining! They then spoke about cultivating steady spiritual habits, and it was suggested he go to tell his girl all about this experience. Not only was their wedding on a high spiritual level, but the course of their married life has been changed beyond question. He even said he was quite open to going into full-time Christian service, if that should be God's will. Traveled a long way, hadn't he, in a few weeks?

One of the things that strikes one most is the relatively small amount of time and effort that may have to be spent with a person to change his whole outlook and even his personality. What we are dealing with is seed, which when it strikes root spreads and grows; what we are dealing with is leaven, which when it finds lodgment in meal distributes itself and grows by what it feeds on.

What, then, are the underlying principles in stories like these? There seem to be four:

1. There must be a *desire*. Whether this arises from conscious and already existent need, or whether it is evoked by exposure to some kind of vital Christian personality or work or company, until a person is eager for what we want him to have,

we cannot get him to take it. It is for us to learn a new ingenuity in finding ways to spark people's imaginations. Many of us live in a climate of religion which is mostly composed of abstract ideas, or impossibly high ideals. We dream of a kingdom to come, deeply aware that it has not yet decisively begun to come even in our own hearts, because we are remote from the actual thoughts, desires, hopes, temptations, and living situations where our people find themselves. Some Christians are close to God, but remote from people; some are close to people, but remote from God; some are close to neither; and *some are close to both*. Those who are near to God and to their fellows are the real fishers of men. Such men and women can inspire a desire for more faith, more dynamic and effective faith, in other people, so that they begin reaching out to find it.

2. There must be *honesty.* We must face our part in our own misfortunes. Even the most unfavoring circumstances, the most apparent tragedies, have in them the possibilities of faith and triumph, if we meet them in the right way. Almost all the suffering in the world could be lessened if not removed, were people only willing to admit their own share in their misfortunes. This requires a great, costly, all-inclusive honesty, sometimes impossible until a man has been caught in his sins and made to suffer for them; or it may come through his seeing the writing on the wall, and being willing to be honest with himself in time. This may also require that we confess to another human being: it is hard to be drastically honest with oneself, not to fool oneself; and this may not touch the root of pride which is the real and deepest trouble always. If we can work the thing out between God and ourselves alone, we escape the shattering necessity to let another human being

know how bad we are. But Protestantism often misses a great spiritual and psychological truth when it tells people they can "go straight to God with their sins"; Catholicism and psychiatry alike know the value, nay, the necessity, of honesty with someone else, as a kind of seal to one's honesty with God and his own soul.

3. There must be *decision*. Much spiritual aspiration vaporizes into wasted emotion because it is not tied down to a decision. We must relinquish our sins, and leave them with God; this is an act, not a desire—a final, irrevocable act. If we slip back, we must make it again. One day it will hold for good. Therefore a decision must have *moral content*. Many people in despair throw themselves down beside their beds, or kneel in a quiet church, and say, "O God, take my life." But they do not specifically hand Him the part that is now causing them anguish—the wrong relation, the hate, the resentment, the fear—and so the prayer never comes to anything. When a man decides to follow Christ, it is not unlike the decision to go to Europe to live: certain ties have to be cut forever, certain things left behind, certain others taken with us, but the break must be complete. It does not mean merely a little polishing off here and there, dusting off a fault, or abstaining from an indulgence—it means a New Life. Let us not take the step till we are ready for it—if we do it prematurely, we shall dull the edge of the issue, and it will be harder to face later on. What is the trouble with most Christians? Little decisions limply made, easily forgotten, impacted and multiplied till one can hardly get them to see the line between white and black, between faith and sin, between Christ and self. We must help to

indicate that line to people, and then help them to step across it with determination.

4. There must be *trust*. They walk out the door the same persons that came in, with the same problems to meet and face, and with the same tendencies to overcome. The difference is entirely within, and it is entirely of God's making. What happened was emotional, ephemeral, transient—or it was the lifelong set of the will Godward. From now on everything depends upon their trusting God *to have worked the miracle*. It is a betrayal of the very decision they made to entertain negative or distrustful thoughts about it, the decision itself involves the attitude of trust. And as we trust, we find our faith is borne out. "According to thy faith be it done unto thee"—it is an inexorable law. The initial experience, with or without much emotion (it is of no consequence), was a glimpse into reality, a touch with and from Almighty God, a sign of what life can and is meant to be. It is as if we saw from far a mountaintop, and said, "There is where I want to go." Then we plunge into the forest at its base, and climb the dark and winding path, knowing that the peak which we saw a while ago is shining there at the top, whether we can now see it or not. We walk onward and upward in trust. We are getting nearer to it every minute we climb!

CHAPTER III

Making Faith Real to People

A MAN once said to me, "You do not need to create a market for your wares; everybody wants the thing you are talking about." This is a good point to remember as we seek to make our faith real to others. Some of them have been "put off" by the wrong kind of religion, or the right kind brought to them in the wrong way; others are not yet awakened to the possibilities of faith, because they have never anywhere been exposed to faith that is alive and running in high gear. But the hunger is there—in everybody. When we talk about our faith, we are not lugging in something extraneous to life, or superfluous: we are seeking to let them in on life's great, open secret.

It is a very natural thing for most people to talk about their enthusiasms. If one loves his garden, or his horse, if one reads a good book or sees a good play or hears a good story, his friends may expect to hear about them. Strangers become friends as they strike interests in common. This is done as one of them sends up a trial balloon. It was never easier to start a conversation about religion than it is today. The self-conscious period, when people discussed it in muffled tones, is now largely past. The magazines, the newspapers and the radio are full of religion, and never before could individuals talk more naturally and freely about it.

If we are to make faith real to individuals, it must be real to us, and what we say of it must flow out of us as naturally as laughter or interest in our work. Many of us put religion in one category, and life in another; when we mention faith, or get ready to do so, we become tense and self-conscious—we go into another gear and stop being natural. This really means that we ourselves are not at home in the outlook of faith. It often means that, while we ourselves may believe strongly, and back the institutions which stand for faith, nothing very dynamic has ever happened to us, and therefore we can speak only in a general way, or in a dull one, about it. We begin to be articulate about our faith when we step out of the spectator's seat, when we get down off the bank and into the stream of grace itself—that current which takes its rise in the loving heart of God, which gathers in people as it moves across the world, and which permits them the unspeakable privilege and joy of sharing with God in the work of creation and redemption. Until something has happened to us, we have little or nothing to say to other people. And this is why so many church people are mute when it comes to making their faith alive to others. It is still too much a matter of static attitude, not enough of dynamic experience, discovery and joy.

Not alone must faith be real to us: we must increasingly understand other people. Here, for example, is a man who had fooled himself for so long with rationalizations that he was in danger of escaping from the realities of life altogether. There seemed to be a line running right down through the middle of his life—a magic dividing line—on one side of which there was written in red: "Dishonesty with oneself, not facing the facts, dodging moral issues, rejecting the promptings of the Inner Voice—this is the beginning of the negative course. Then follows confusion, nothing black or white, everything muddy and gray, no standards of moorings left, only a strong desire to have one's own way, and pursue it unhindered. The wedge of conflict is steadily pushed in deeper and deeper, till the inner pressure becomes almost unbearable. One grows more and more lonely, separated and afraid. The family may notice this, or a close friend, and seek to get through the wall to us, but is rebuffed—we are determined to handle it ourselves. Physical symptoms of sickness may begin to appear—aches and pains, fatigue and listlessness. One seeks refuge and release in reading, play, exercise, sleep, drugs, more work, but it is only temporary and one must come back to the old grind, with the divided self the most prominent thing in one's consciousness. Sleep is fitful, one wakens at early hours, startled, wide-awake, bedeviled and hagridden by anxious, futile thoughts. Relationships turn dry, work suffers, and life is a burden. There are but two possible ends to this list: breakdown, perhaps suicide, which one takes because there seems to be no other way; or cutting loose from the dreadful circle by a thorough-going honesty." There is not one of us who has not at some time been on the red side of the dividing line, and that is where most people who have come to the mental and emotional logic of our modern feverishness and unbelief find themselves today. Thoreau said that "most men live lives of quiet desperation." This is true beneath the surface, however much or little it shows above it.

And on the other side of the dividing line, there was written in black: "Honesty with oneself, facing all the facts, including the worst, not minimizing what has been really wrong, letting the Holy Spirit cut down with clean conviction, like a drill through concrete. Keeping the channel open to the Inner Voice, by which God drops into our minds the bits of truth which we need to hear. The moment an issue for decision arises, it sorts itself: if a course of action is wrong, one puts it from his mind, thus finding moral clarity, with a great saving of effort and struggle as a consequence. In place of conflict, there comes a great sense of inward peace and rightness. One feels in harmony with the universe, with the order of things, with God, with people. Relationships take on a tingle again, one begins enjoying people, feeling in touch and sympathy with them once more. When one of them seeks to be real with us, and comes behind the barriers, he is welcomed, for no longer have we anything to hide. Pride gives way to a great, happy sense of dependence on others, on God, on the goodness of life itself. Often the aches and pains go away by themselves, for they were the fruit of conflict and inner strife. One sleeps soundly, wakens happy, goes to work with a song in his heart. Life, instead of a burden, becomes an unspeakable blessing and privilege. One is thankful once more that he was born." This is the freedom that is open to the person who truly finds God and faith. "Where the Spirit of the Lord is, there is liberty" (II Corinthians 3:17). When we try to make faith real to people, we seek to help them shift their lives from the red to the black side of that dividing line.

Everything turns on thoroughgoing honesty with oneself. Most of us, if we pay our bills, do not lie like troopers, nor take what does not belong to us, call ourselves honest. But there is a far more costly honesty with oneself and about oneself which is the beginning of wisdom. Science and the pursuit of "objective" truth may be many a person's escape from that much more costly, difficult and necessary honesty about himself. We take the kindly and complimentary things our friends say about us as truth; we are confirmed in our good opinion of ourselves. So we become satisfied, and dishonest, and go spiritually dead. It usually takes either a crisis in our affairs (a threatened divorce, a family row, a spell of "nerves") to reveal to us what we really are, or else the kindly intervention of another person. We must learn to collide in a creative way with many good but self-righteous and self-deceived persons, and help them to see themselves as they really are. Most conventional folk, and most Protestants, are brought up with the idea that there is no need to "bare one's soul" to another person: if we need any help, we shall go straight to God. Do we not perceive the lurking pride that lies in this—"I can paddle my own canoe, with a little help from the Almighty"? We *may* be able to handle the problem that confronts us; but this will never handle the pride that underlies the whole of our life. It is this very self-reliance, this fancied adequacy, this complacency that we ourselves are competent to handle our lives, that is the real trouble with us. Only after we have had the courage to go and blurt out what is really the matter, to a clergyman or other honest and trusted spiritual counselor, and the sometimes devastating process of opening our inner lives is behind us, shall we know either what true honesty means, or enjoy the intense relief that comes through its exercise. We must increasingly learn how to be the recipients of these confidences, to keep them inviolate, and to work through them to an answer.

Now for some steps by which we come to this place with people:

The first step, in making faith real to others, is to *make friends.* A story may illustrate. A woman deeply interested in personal religion asked two of her spiritual friends to dine with her husband who was only conventionally interested in the Church. He was expecting to be "set upon" by them, and was a little terrified. There was in the wife too much the feeling that they were "ganging up" with her to persuade him—and that is a very good setup to defeat what one wants to accomplish. They realized they had to get on *his* side. One of them risked a wink and a sly dig at wives that push men around. They found he was intensely interested in horses, so they talked riding for about half an hour—that is, he did, for this gave him a chance to stave off the terrible moment when they might "begin." They discovered that he was much interested in politics, and drew the conversation around to the relation between freedom and faith, to the statements of some of the Founding Fathers and pioneers about the place of religion in national life (like William Penn's wonderful aphorism, "Men must be governed by God or they will be ruled by tyrants"). By the end of the evening, he was "with" them to the hilt, asking questions, seeking to discover ways by which he could co-operate and help make all this live for other people. The obvious principle is: don't begin talking about religion till you have won the other person's confidence, and he is taking some initiative in the conversation. This may come in the first five minutes, or you may have to wait months or years for it. You can not force the issue, nor push too fast without disaster. Keep living out a real friendship and relationship all the while.

The second step is to wait for a place in the natural conversation where you can easily *speak about your own faith.*

Let us say the conversation turns to Russia—how shall we get back to faith? Well, we can't yet get behind the iron curtain with Christian and democratic ideas, can we? Therefore we must deal with what we *can* reach, the border nations that are on the fence whether to go the democratic or the communistic way, mustn't we? But everything depends on how America treats those nations, and what they think of America as the most potent democratic nation in the world. And how America treats them depends on what America really is. The jitter-bugging, gadget-buying, lynch-condoning, self-indulgent, divided and materialistic America will convince and "sell" nobody. But there is an America that loves fair play, honest dealing, consideration for the other fellow, real freedom and faith in God, that will draw any nation to imitation. This America, however, depends on those with faith, those who are themselves putting their lives into obeying the will of God, and are not willing to be what Clare Booth Luce calls "Christian coupon clippers on the original investment made by our fore-fathers." And the situation is right back in our own laps! What we say of our own faith must be relevant to the general conversation, not dragged in. It must not be dogmatic nor self-assertive, but as if we were simply thinking aloud. It must concern things that have happened, as well as general statements; for an ounce of event is worth a ton of preachment. We must not let it get too much into the upper ether of argument, but keep it on the ground of facts, events. We must learn to discover the universal elements in our own and others' experiences and emphasize them, rather than the merely individual factors: in discussing St. Paul's conversion, for instance, we would not emphasize the blinding light and the loss of sight and the supernatural vision of Jesus which was given to him, out rather that when he lay prostrate in the dust of that Damascus Road he said something we all need to say in some terms or other, "Lord, what wilt thou have me to do?" (Acts 9:6). That was his self-surrender, his part in his own conversion; and it indicates ours. Professor Hocking says a profound thing, "We find that religion becomes universal at the same time that it becomes most peculiarly personal. . . ." We must not fear, then, to say what is real and personal to us. There is a way of speaking about one's own faith that puts a chasm between oneself and others without faith, as if we were specially wise or good or righteous; but there is a way of speaking about it that makes the other person hungry for it! Keep on his side all the time, emotionally even if you must say something from which intellectually he dissents. St. Ignatius Loyola said, "The greatest vigilance must be used to banish all desire of triumph."

The third step is to find a point of *need*. Many well-adjusted people, with little sense of personal need, will best be reached by their concern for the need of the community, the nation, the Church, the world—or even a person in trouble. If this concern is more than an emotional one, they will be doing something about it, and we may find them already teammates with us in some cause that needs help. If they are doing nothing, or if what they do is ineffective, it may point to a need in themselves of which they have been but dimly aware. Spiritual ineffectiveness is perhaps the great need of the reputable and believing people. If we cannot get over to others a thing as glorious and much-needed as faith in God and in Jesus Christ, there is something lacking in our faith. Love, prayer, sympathy, being with people and serving them in obvious ways, will often disclose their deeper needs to us. Most individuals would give anything if they could find someone with whom they could open up the real needs of their lives, and talk about them fully and frankly. The majority of people like to talk about themselves, but usually do it fruitlessly.

Any touch with people may set off a spiritual miracle. For instance, a man dropped into the house to sell a garbage burner. I asked him to sit down. His name was familiar—was he related to so-and-so? Yes—he was a cousin, "but we never speak." This is open sesame for a talk about human relations, about the way in which confessing the other person's sins leads to war, while confessing one's own leads to peace. "That cuts in on pride, doesn't it?" Yes, it does; and therefore we need the help of God to do it. Noticing a redness about his face, the thought that he might be an alcoholic came to me. I mentioned Alcoholics Anonymous[1]—yes, he knew them, had been to meetings, they had something, but he was not going now. "Having victory over the stuff now, are you?" No, not steadily. We talked about deep honesty concerning oneself, and how the failure to be honest leads on to so much else—broken relations, running away, infidelity, resentment, and back again to drink. This touched him, and he opened up on just what was going on—some things he had told no one else. It brought him back to honesty, back to A.A., and back to his real self. Our questions must not be too direct, nor yet too general. We must be, not critics, but fellow sinners at all times. One does not say to an alcoholic, "Of course, I have never had your prob-

[1] See pp. 78-80 for a fuller discussion of the program of Alcoholics Anonymous.

lem." One says rather, "Well, you get drunk on gin and whiskey: I am more apt to get drunk on fear, or criticism, or gossip."

Occasionally the need is some kind of outward trouble or sorrow. A man who has come victoriously through a great deal of trouble, says, "God gives man two great gifts: the gift of faith, and the gift of adversity." One learns to thank God for the adversity which strips us of self-dependence. There are times when, in sheer mercy, God picks us up like a ball, and tosses us whither He will—rolls us like a stone in a stream till the rough edges are worn off—lets us suffer contempt and agony if it will restore our souls and bring us back to Himself. Now such times are open times for His Spirit to work in men's lives. If we come to people at these times with genuine sympathy, we can go on to the expression of real faith, and they are specially sensitive to the need of it when their lives are in difficulty. After all, who else can really say anything where death has struck, except a Christian who believes in God and in everlasting life? The rest can be sympathetic, but tragedy is the last word. For us, hope and faith are the last words!

The fourth step is to *be a good listener*. Many clergymen tend to carry on their sermonizing out of the pulpit and do all the talking. It is fatal. The most important thing is, not that we be sure to get across what we have to say, but that we succeed in getting the person's mind open to what we may have to say. The best way to get them to listen to us later on is to listen to them first. Get them going on what interests them—they will reveal themselves by it. The old adage says, the best way to stop a runaway horse is to run with him. Somewhere we must say enough to intrigue them about faith, and open up a need; after that, once the interest is roused, we do well to be silent for much of the time, only putting in a word here and there to help on the story, or uttering what someone called a "sympathetic grunt" every now and then to indicate easy interest and understanding. There is an immense healing in letting the story come out as it will, as every psychiatrist, good counselor, and well-versed priest or pastor knows; if it were allowed to come out earlier with some of the family, a trusted minister or other friend, it might never need to get to a psychiatrist at all. It is sometimes difficult for people to talk about what concerns them most, and we must be creatively attentive, unsentimentally sympathetic, and at times almost impersonal, as though we happened to be a kind of listening-post for life and the universe, where healing truth might safely come out. Others will need to be helped about "total recall" who should not, at least more than once, be allowed to go over the whole story in detail, though we shall sometimes find that deeply troubled persons need to say what is on their hearts no matter how often this has to be done, for it is the only mode of relief and of healing. This time of listening should give us opportunity for two things: (1) continuous prayer to God that we may be led by Him in every move we make, every thought and emotion we have, and (2) the chance to understand what kind of person this is, watching for characteristics like ambition, temper, neurotic tendencies, willfullness, insecurity, self-indulgence, etc.

The fifth step is to *suggest the answer*. People muff many problems because they bring self into them, and leave God out of them. When God goes to work on a human situation, coming to it through the human faith of the person who faces it, a whole new and creative factor enters in. We may want to point out that there are always two factors in every problem: there is the situation, and there is the way we meet and react to that situation. The second is more important than the first; life takes care of the first, but we take care of the second, or should. Whether an event shall bless or curse us lies, not so much in the nature of the event, as in the nature of our reception of the event. Faith mixed with a problem is what often turns a mess into a miracle. When God enters a situation, the moral issues clear. We stop looking for self-justification, and look for truth. We see where we have been wrong, and are eager to make it right—this may be the first step in a miraculous progress.

A man sought help who had wasted his life completely, a son of privilege who had become a prodigal in earnest. He was bitter against some people to whom he had gone for help, and who had been honest enough to tell him that he did not really mean business nor want to be helped by being changed. He said they had "thrown him out" and added bitterness to his other defeats. It was pointed out to him that he was blaming them for his own failures, and he admitted it. He needed encouragement, many people do, and his counselor poured out real concern for him, without sentimentally playing Providence to him by giving him money. Faith sets alight faith in another life: with a smile of recognition he laid hold of a new hope. In prayer he sealed a decision. He went back to his family in honesty, and to the group he said had "thrown him out," and straightened out both relations. Prayer has become a great bulwark in his life. A bit later he left a note which said, "Have just been round the corner in church, having a chat with my new Friend. He gets easier to talk to all the time." I say we must "suggest" the answer, because the person can only find and choose the answer for himself—counseling which dominates and coerces another, by too much salesmanship and "personality," is malpractice. Sometimes, near the crisis, one may say, "It's your decision, remember, not mine—don't do it unless you mean it."

The true answer, the final and all-inclusive answer, of course, is to be found in Jesus Christ alone. Said Dr. Adolph Harnack, "Here is a religion which embraces everything. And yet it can always be expressed with absolute simplicity: one name, the name of Jesus Christ, still sums up everything." And Dr. Farmer calls Christianity "the awareness of the living God in Christ as absolute demand and final succor." People are in all kinds of stages of belief about Christ, some still reacting against childhood overdoses of religion (they get to be childish themselves when they keep up this excuse too long); some thinking of Him as merely an idyllic Figure walking poetically through the fields of Galilee long ago; some only considering Him the best life ever lived (which is untenable in the light of His stupendous claims about Himself, which must be true or false; and if true, they constitute the grounds for His "absolute demand" upon us); some only looking upon Him as no more than the sum of orthodox opinions, with all the right titles and qualities, but none of the real power and glory. Yet others in the light of all that He is and claims and has done are ready to say with St. Thomas, "My Lord and my God." People move into deeper theological conceptions, not alone by further study and knowledge, but by richer spiritual experiences, by being brought into the chain of events which flow from a full faith. When the deeper experience is encouraged, it may take a deeper faith and theology to interpret it.

The sixth step is to *encourage decision*. Many a conversation about religion vaporizes into an emotional memory, or even less, because it comes to no concrete conclusions. There will be some moral decisions which should be reached. A man living in sin with a woman not his wife must be prepared to give her up—not to throw her off irresponsibly, for he ought to seek to make his new decision a challenge that she make the same one—but the relationship will be wholly different. A financial debt will be acknowledged, and a promise made to pay it off as rapidly as possible, the dates and amounts being agreed upon. A relationship in which bitterness has existed needs honest confession all around, and this somebody must start who sees the moral point, taking the risk of confession whether the other person reciprocates or not. We must be right with men, if we are to be right with God—and vice versa. For this reason, in every decision to give up a particular sin or evil, there must be also the more inclusive decision to give up the whole self in surrender to God and His will—for the evil to which we have clung means also a divided, unconverted self to which we have clung, and which has thus denied and defied God. If we give God our innermost hearts and selves, our sins will drop off like dead leaves.

Decision should also include taking on steady devotional habits. We need to continue and deepen the New Life which we are beginning. Time must be set aside for this, the first half hour of the day being the best time to begin. It will include the Bible, some other devotional reading, and prayer. It will include linking up with the church of our choice and loyalty, going regularly, and taking full responsibility in its life and work. Decision should also mean examining one's life investment, with a view to fulfilling the great command, "Seek ye first the kingdom of

God, and his righteousness. . . ." Are our lives pitched to that level? Are we ready to have them pitched there? Some of us are in the wrong work; it is too materialistic, too selfish, too comfortable and easy, and we should consider definite Christian service, at home or overseas. Others must stay where they are, but lift the level of their work to accord with their new spiritual commitment, according to the suggestions found in the next two chapters. All should feel a responsibility to make real to other individuals the faith that is their own most precious possession, and pray God to use them to this end. For the whole Christian enterprise has risen and spread through the world because men who have been given faith felt a responsibility to share that faith with others. We shall never know how much or how little faith we have till we start to give it away. And we shall never know anything like its full joy and adventure till we have let God use us to make it real to another human being.[2]

A young business woman to whom Christ had become a great reality through her church was wishing that she might impart some of this same faith to her roommate. This is her account of the way in which it came about:

"It will never cease to amaze me (nor will it anyone, I suppose, who is in touch with God) to see the way in which He

[2] NOTE: Nothing specific is said in this book about helping those who are mentally or emotionally sick. It will be well to consult their physician and to work with him. I refer the reader to a chapter in my book *How You Can Help Other People* on dealing with the mentally sick. Consider also this paragraph from Dr. Fritz Kunkel (*In Search of Maturity,* p. 17), "People with character difficulties, moral deviations and vices, are sent to doctors as though they were sick. The physical and mental diseases certainly belong to the realm of medicine, and therefore ethical evaluation in these cases must be avoided. But if vices are diseases, they cease to be vices; and theology, sending the drunkard and the gambler to the physician, relinquishes its last connection with reality: the ethical task."

works sometimes. One night last week I was debating with myself whether to go to a recital or not. I wanted to hear the
music, yet something kept driving me on home. I was tired.
God can use tired feet in wondrous ways, as I have found out.
On arriving at home, I found my roommate F—— in the
apartment alone in a somewhat discouraged mood. She was
dead tired from school and work, hungry, felt that she was
wandering aimlessly and getting nowhere, just marking time.
All summer long I have wanted to help F——. She is a sweet
girl with a warm, generous personality, many friends, a grand
disposition, a goodly amount of brains, and all the nicer at-
tributes of gracious living. She has no major personality
problems, but she knows her life falls short of the best. She
'discourages' easily, and seems to have no incentive that makes
life an adventure. She likes life most of the time, and doesn't
feel despondent, but it does fall short of what it might be. I
knew she was tired last night, so I suggested dinner at home
—not solely for her benefit, for I was tired too. At dinner we
began talking rather seriously about her feeling of discouragement and aimlessness. She has known all along what my religion means to me but has never inquired much about it. Nor
did she take the initiative that night. I merely began to point
out that I had once reached the same place she is reaching
right now, and that the only thing that seemed to make sense
was finally getting in touch with God, finding out that He is
personally interested in every single thing about me, and wants
to help me much more than I ever sought to have His help.
I told her various reasons why I came finally to believe in and
know the power of prayer. That talk began about 8:00 P.M.
and at 2:30 A.M. we were still talking. I read her several stories

of transformed people, and told her how one girl had come through to real faith. Well, a glorious thing has happened. She had always thought it would be so complicated to find God. I simply suggested that she turn over as much of her life as she could to as much of God as she could understand. She made the experiment. Her nerves which earlier in the evening were completely "shot" were just as completely relaxed later. We have several fine books around the apartment, some of C. S. Lewis'. Up to this time she had no desire even to look at those books. But she said, 'I have a million things to do to get ready for school, but right now all I want to do is to read one of those books.' I found her in bed reading when we stopped talking. She said, 'I think talking to you and reading this may well be the most important thing I've ever done.' Next morning, even after so few hours of sleep, we both felt wonderful, and she told me she never had had such a good outlook before— she thinks things will never bother her again as they used to. . . . Funny, isn't it?—I thought I had been slipping on F—— because I hadn't been able quite to reach her need. It all proves that God has His time for doing things, and all we can hope to do is to trust and obey. . . . P.S. Suppose I had gone to the recital?"

Will you note several things about that story which are of general usefulness and importance in making faith real to individuals? She let God guide her to the place where He wanted her to be, by natural factors like "tired feet" and by the inward prompting. She had been wanting to help her friend, waiting for an opportunity, and was alert to it when it arose. She had sensed the need before. She did a natural, human thing like suggesting they have dinner together. The conversation swung

to her friend's problem and they talked about it. Then it was
time to witness herself to what faith meant to her in meeting
a similar problem. She knew stories to tell her of others who
had found faith. She helped her to start a spiritual experiment.
Since that time, she has related her to other people who are
finding the same adventure of faith, so that she may have fellowship in the new life, and begin to take her share in the life
and work of the Church and bringing yet others to the joyous
adventure of walking with God in trust and obedience.

CHAPTER IV

Making Faith Work in Situations

THE Christian religion began with a great fact. St. John says this was the great fact: "And the Word was made flesh" (St. John 1:14). All the mystery and the greatness and the power of God were cut down to human shape and size in Jesus Christ; so that man no longer had to wonder and grope for God, he had but to look right at Jesus. "He that hath seen me hath seen the Father" (St. John 14:9). God, in order to make Himself better understood, incarnated Himself in Jesus. "And the Word was made flesh."

It sometimes seems as if the churches and the preachers exactly reverse that process, so that "the flesh is made word," the simple, practical, working Gospel is vaporized and etherealized into words till it becomes lost in generalization. Many a parson could confess his sins in this doggerel:

> I live in a sea of words,
> Where the nouns and the adjectives flow;
> And the verbs speak of action that never takes place,
> And the sentences come and go.

The Church cannot merely convert individuals: it must convert social relations, groups, society, nations and the world. Christian conversion begins with individuals, for in the wills of men take place those inner events that so largely determine outer events. There has never been found, there never will be found, any substitute for the individual search for, and discovery by, God: we must travel a path that in part at least is single and solitary. But individuals apart from relations do not exist, and unless relationships receive the effect of individual conversion, and are themselves converted, religion is a private and selfish affair. Moreover, organized relationships, which are essential in an ordered society, arrange themselves into institutions; and these, too, must increasingly show the effects of the convertedness of the individuals who manage them. It is easier to convert a relationship, to find fellowship with someone of another race, or party, with whom one would not ordinarily have fellowship, and to Christianize the immediate contact with another human being or small company of human beings, than it is to convert an institution which is a series of complicated relations that have hardened into patterns that are much more difficult to break, though not impossible. Christianity must tackle the Christianization of individuals, of relationships, and of institutions. We can no longer stand aside and beg the practical question, say of business or of politics, because we want to keep our skirts clean. Nor can we beg the question by espousing merely some one partial cause, as if the whole Kingdom were wrapped in it (e.g., Prohibition, pacifism and many ostensibly socially idealistic schemes). We must seriously attempt the conversion of those relations and institutions which characterize our society. We must learn how to practice what might be called "situational evangelism."

Here is the supreme opportunity of the layman. There is a great cry among the clergy today about the importance of laymen's work in evangelism. Some of this is sheer "passing the buck." The clergy are not doing it themselves, are inept and inexperienced and uncomfortable with it, and the hue and cry about "laymen" is an attempt to put the responsibility on someone else because they shirk it themselves. Clergy who will do this work themselves, and *lead* their laymen in it, are convincing; clergy who attempt to *push* their laymen into it, when they will not learn to do it themselves, are first-water "buckpassers." Yet the importance of lay-work is there. These men and women are in direct touch with the wheels on which society runs. They see it more at firsthand than ministers do, and have a responsibility for daily decisions which, rightly made, are the path along which the Spirit of God can come into that business, that factory, that farm, that institution. Sabatier says, "It is not easy to hear and apply to oneself the exhortations of preachers who, aloft in the pulpit, seem to be carrying out a mere formality; it is just as difficult to escape from the appeals of a layman who walks at our side." William Temple summed it all up well for us when he said, "The man outside feels differently, and to him the lay witness is most effective. We must move nearer to a state of affairs where the minister stands for the things of God before the congregation while the congregation stands for the things of God before the outside world." The minister himself needs to be in touch with that "outside world," however, else what he says in the pulpit cannot have genuine relevance for the congregation as they try to "stand for the things of God" before it. The layman rightly wishes to speak mostly through what he does: if he is applying Christian principle in his business relations, he feels sincere and natural when he talks about how it affects business; but if he is not doing this, to speak personally of his faith is hypocritical, and he rightly avoids it. We must never forget that many, perhaps most, well-adjusted and healthy-minded and conventional people will be better convinced and moved by seeing Christianity at work in a situation than by being told what they ought to do about it. Again, an ounce of demonstration and instance is worth a ton of generalized advice.

Let us begin with *business*. And let "the Word be made flesh" at once, in some concrete illustrations.

A boiler-room superintendent in a public utility plant was in charge of a crew of eighty rough, tough and profane men. The fact that they came from seven or eight different countries only served to aggravate the disputes and fights that arose. Weighing about two hundred and fifty pounds this man ruled with an iron hand, matching his temper against theirs. When he accepted Christ he began feeling that this was not quite good enough. He began talking with his men in a friendly way, creating confidence in them instead of fear and competition. He began having little "get-togethers" at noon, when they talked over matters in the plant, and even their own personal problems. The control his faith had brought him relayed itself to them. Their relations improved, their work improved, dirty and profane talk disappeared, there was not a single industrial accident in that plant for seven years after!

An advertising man in New York found an experience of God that changed his personal and family life. He knew it should change his business, too. How to begin? He talked with one or two of the employes privately, at lunch and other times, raising with them the question of a daily "get-together' in the office before the day started. It was to be entirely voluntary, no one was expected to come unless he wanted to, nor forced to take part if he did. They tried it beginning twelve years ago. Every morning a group meets in the office at eight thirty instead of nine. A good proportion of the employes come. They read the Bible for a while, they bring up problems and questions of policy, they are quiet in prayer before God, or vocal, as they feel led to be. It is almost a strainless office, where more than one person *has found God* just by going there to work.

A young lawyer was consulted about a divorce by the wife of a man returning from overseas—she was, she thought, in love with someone else. The lawyer got to work on the case. But that night, at home, he was praying about it; and he felt God was not satisfied with what he planned to do, and that he should make an attempt to reconcile them instead. Next day, when he saw the wife, he told her about what had happened to him the night before; and he reminded her of the solemn vows she had taken, of the cruel selfishness of greeting her husband with a letter saying she wanted a divorce. He spoke frankly of how God can change situations through changing the people in them. She thought it over, reconsidered, decided against the divorce, and went to the coast to meet her husband! There are many people who need to hear some simple advice: Don't divorce your husband or wife—divorce your sins instead!

Melvin Evans, of Chicago, says, in his splendid little book *It Works,* which he calls "human engineering—a plan for industrial peace," that "the major factor in business success is not methods or materials but MEN." You will find admirable stories of the practical application of Christianity to business in Mr. Evans' book, e.g., on pages 140-41, and 178-79; and a set of unbeatable rules to govern such application on pages 190-91.

The layman whose personal story we told on pages 9-11 tells of how he began to relate his faith to his business:

"Some time ago I read a book by General Dobbie. As I read, I thought if he could withstand the Siege of Malta and have faith that God would see him through, it was asinine to feel that He would not help me if I really tried to serve Him in my business. On a trip last summer, I talked to an assistant vice-president of our company about General Dobbie's book, and suggested that God certainly had some plans which He expected Christian people to carry out in industry. I asked what he would think of the possibility of forming a group in our company to explore the idea. Much to my delight, I found him in accord, so we decided when our vacation was over, we would see what we could do about it. I bought some of General Dobbie's books and gave them to eight of our associates, asking them to read the book so that we might discuss the contents at a later date. In September the assistant vice-president and I decided we would ask the seven others to meet with us one evening. We gathered in a hotel room—the very same place where I'd done some fancy drinking in days gone by. There we organized our group. All of the men but one were in accord with trying what we had in mind. Another said he must be frank, he couldn't quite see it all, but would like to explore the idea. About nine o'clock, I asked if they would mind if we had a prayer. I offered a prayer and the group was launched.

"In November we met again. Several of the men said the effect of the first meeting on them had been very great, and had broken down rival feelings between some of them. At this meeting we discussed further what might be done in our business life to bring it fully into accord with our Christian faith. One man told of an incident that had occurred in one of his plants. He was a general superintendent: he told us he had prayed about a bad situation, and the help he received from God resulted in a fine solution. We had some more prayer at this meeting. We met again in December and had as visitor a vice-president and general manager of one of our subsidiary companies, who is a Christian and made a fine contribution in what he said. A couple of men in the group prayed. We brought up several questions relating to matters we thought needed improvement. I had a feeling I should say nothing about a further meeting, and did not. Two months passed, and no meeting. One day I was talking with one of our group, and he raised the question about another meeting. I said I did not want to press them, if the fellows did not want it. He said, 'You can't stop them now!' At the next meeting, one of the men reviewed Melvin Evans' book, which I bought after hearing him speak: the review was so stimulating that we had to get copies for the whole group! At our last meeting one of the general superintendents led, and opened with a passage of Scripture which he used as the basis for some very constructive suggestions.

"This is not, you understand, an official company group, and does not necessarily evidence company policy; but it is made up of men who because of their positions necessarily influence policy to a large degree, particularly as they have to do with personnel, or so-called employer-employee relationships. It consists of an assistant manufacturing vice-president, three general superintendents, four managers of staff departments, and a vice-president. . . . With the conviction now that our problems, whether they be personal, family, political, social or otherwise, will only progress as God guides our lives, individually and collectively, I for one intend to carry on as best I can as a soldier of Christ in industry. If I run up against somebody who doesn't like it, that will be too bad! There are eight men associated with me in this experiment who believe in what we are doing and expect to get help, not only with our own problems, but also in formulating policies that will be good for the whole company, or as I prefer to say 'family.' With this in mind, we are going ahead."

There will, of course, be some who "do not like it," who want business on the old, piratical, dog-eat-dog, dishonest basis. Most companies will be open to such a reasonable and practical approach as this man has made. On the other hand, there will be business which resists all change and improvement. A woman whom I know found herself working for a company with a public relations account that might affect adversely American foreign policy. She remonstrated quietly, but got nowhere. She was not, as a Christian, going to take a salary for telling lies of a dangerous international character, and there was nothing to do but resign. We must take that risk: the challenge may not be accepted. There is place for the prophet, and for prophetic failure. But resigning is a last resort: better far, if possible, the courageous, patient labor of changing the situation from within by changing the people, and their mutual relations, that make the situation.

Let us turn to politics, and to some concrete illustrations.

A lawyer in middle life found himself with a little time on his hands, and a great concern for the corrupt politics of his state. He began to work in the state committee of his party. After a time, they made him treasurer. This gave him opportunity to change the situation which had made it so expensive for a man to run for high office that only men of wealth, or backed by groups with a special ax to grind, could usually be elected. He raised money in small amounts from many sources, which made it possible for the party to back fit men for office. He made friends with the governor, who was of the other party, and co-operated with him where his policies were for the best interests of the state. In all this he was quite disinterested, and had no idea of ever running for office himself. But this kind of unselfish integrity wins confidence, and constitutes the kind of leadership which the people want. When a vacancy occurred in the office of United States Senator, he was urged to run himself for the office. He hesitated—would it queer what he had done for the sake of the state, and look as if he wanted something for himself all the time? He was prevailed upon to run, however, and was elected; and when he was returned to the Senate for a second term, it was with the highest majority ever given anyone but a presidential candidate in his state. A man of prayer, he belongs to a small company of senators who meet weekly for prayer, fellowship and counsel. He has learned the secret of triangular human relationships, with God at the apex, and two men, two groups, two points of view, at the base. The two may be at irreconcilable loggerheads on their own level, but as they take higher ground, they tend to come together. You know the old adage: "Your way, my way, and the right way"? Somebody has got to represent God's way, right in the ruck of daily politics. Many instances of where this has happened are naturally of a confidential nature; but they are happening right along. One man of this caliber can lift politics from sordid horse-trading to inspired statesmanship. He can give the present-day "wise and honest" a "standard to which they can repair," in George Washington's phrase.

Consider the contrast between two men: Georges Clemenceau at Paris after World War I, getting in his vengeful blows for France, and undercutting all that Woodrow Wilson sought to do. One day Clemenceau said of Wilson, "That man talks like Jesus Christ!" What a pity—what a costly, tragic pity the world did not then heed the man who "talked like Jesus Christ"! And then consider Martin Niemöller face to face with Adolph Hitler. Niemöller was with a group of church leaders on January 25, 1934, when Hitler told them, "Gentlemen, mind your own business, and let me take care of the German nation." One by one Hitler put out his hand to dismiss his visitors, and as Dr. Niemöller held his hand, he said to Hitler, "Mr. Chancellor, God himself has entrusted *us* with the responsibility for our nation, and no power and no authority in the world is entitled to take it from us." Shall the Christian Church remain aloof from politics, as the skeptics and humanists would like it to do—or shall it take up that responsibility with which "God Himself has entrusted" it, and dare to make faith work in that largest and most complicated of institutions, which we call the nation?

But this is not something which can be left to our leaders alone: all of us have responsibility for putting our religion to work in national and international affairs. A letter lies at hand which reads, "We have just returned from India, and have seen at close range what America has been doing in India and China, and what impressions are being made by Americans. It seems to me that our national and international ideals have never been finer—peace, social and economic justice, and feeding a starving world. And I think that the country is really backing all the great humanitarian ideals. But what good can be accomplished when so many of the individual men, in whose hands lies their execution, are venal, corrupt and immoral? Of course there have been many fine soldiers in India, who knew how to behave, but there have been too many of the other sort. And the immorality is not confined to the soldiers or the 'military.' American 'policies' can never eradicate the impressions made by *Americans*!"

Consider the great field of education. How can one person begin to affect an institution? In one of our great universities is a young man of promise and leadership. He is personable, suave, intelligent and practical. "About a year ago," he says, "I was converted though I didn't fully realize it at the time. I had not come to appreciate the fact of the Presence of Christ here and now. His Resurrection was still overshadowed by His Birth. I had then no inkling of the surrender He demands. Later on meeting ——— and coming to ——— and meeting the fine Christians there was for me an important experience. It took me out of myself and demonstrated that Christ not only wants people, but He also wants them to act. The chaplain at college says, 'Don't go into the ministry if you can stay out.' After the Thanksgiving conference I could no longer stay out, and ever since then I have been learning more about what Christ wants me to do. . . . I can see that it will be a long fight, but I have progressed steadily by the Grace of God, and know now that He will give as much help as a man will permit Him to give.

"Knowing men at college like K—— and B—— and N—— and V—— has encouraged me. It is promising that so many men like this are going into the Church, because they are leaders. . . . None of us thinks he can drag people into the fold by our magnetic personalities or by our social charm or by our sartorial magnificence or by any other of the world's standards. . . . It is a *fellowship* we have found together at —— of strong men who are trying to prepare themselves for the service of Christ, and the numbers are not small.

"The column I write in the college paper once a week happened because the chairman of the paper lived across the hall from me. He came into my room one day and asked if there were any 'editorial lights hiding themselves under bushels.' I told him I had always wanted to write a column for the paper, and when he asked what my specialty was, I said, 'religion.' He took me up, and after he had sold the idea to the board, I was off. —— gave me the title and much good criticism, as did my roommates."

One day he said, simply and humbly, that during the previous two months he had had good talks about his faith with his three roommates, the members of his own family, and several others amongst his college friends! He writes, "I have no illusions as to what may have been accomplished among the undergraduates. At the most my rather clumsy attempts to discuss great matters in a light but not frivolous tone may have made a few people think. I know of some that it affected . . . I found in the process of writing that phrases would come into my head uninvited, and that these were at the same time generalized, and also embarrassingly applicable to my own conduct and faith.

I could not criticize the behavior of other people without having some of the criticism stick to me!"

Notice these factors in what he has done on his campus: he was "converted," he got in touch with other Christian men on the campus and formed a fellowship and "team," he let God determine his vocation, he looked for an opportunity to express what he believed through a medium (writing) in which he was somewhat experienced, he talked with individuals, and he kept growing! It is through such men that our educational institutions, so largely born of Christian faith, that have often detoured through materialism and humanism, can be brought back to their original faith. One is grateful for men in faculties who teach Christianity as an intellectually reputable discipline, and for all the organized religious work on our campuses. The outcome of such work should be creative, disciplined, effective personalities like this undergraduate of whom we have been speaking.

Consider also how faith works in the home. Dr. Langmuir says that if children are to grow soundly and well, homes, schools and communities must try to meet the four basic emotional needs in which strong adult personalities depend; she defines these as: to be accepted and loved; to become competent and independent; to become realistic and responsible; and to have faith and serve others. Clearly a living Christian faith will do much toward producing these four needed qualities. But how shall we accomplish it? So many parents want their children to have the fruits and benefits of Christian training, while exempting themselves from the continuing need of it. Children become more aware of God as they see their parents praying, and as they pray with them, than they ever can become through mere teaching, important as this is. And what ethical sanction shall we give them? We tell a child to do thus and so, and he asks why. "Because I say so" may be a valid reason for discipline, but it is not a valid reason to put foundations under the command. Children must know that there is an *objective law,* arising out of the truth and right, which in turn arise in God Himself; and to which all, parents and children alike, are subject and accountable.

Here, for example, are two stalwart young men. They have a natural and passionate love of their home. They have two more brothers—four of them, all big and healthy and muscular and well-adjusted. One day their father, a devoted layman, was asked how he had brought up four such fine boys. "I think the Church's most important job is to bring Christ into the homes of its people," he replied. "In our home, we never had any 'don'ts.' At some meal in the day, when everyone is at home, we have some Bible reading and prayer and some conversation about what we have been reading and about the family plans. The friendship of Jesus Christ is the deepest bond between us." Do not think it has been easy to maintain that standard with four growing lads, exposed to the irreligious and materialism of today's schools and colleges. Yet that family has maintained it. It has not been forced, but from the earliest days it has been accepted as the way that family lives. And they go to chuch together in the same way. Everyone should know Dr. Henry C. Link's discovery, on psychological test, that "among the most important habits contributing to an effective personality are the following: Going to Sunday school and having parents that attend church. The very fact of parents attending church was a factor in the development of desirable personality traits

on the part of the children, and the attendance at Sunday school
by the children was an even more important factor." Let us all
begin again the three habits that create strong Christian homes:
family prayers, family attendance at church, and the children's
attendance at Sunday school.

This brings us to the last situation in which we want to
discuss faith at work. And that is in the church itself. It is the
natural place where people look to find faith at work. Do they
always find it? Have means become ends? Are the minister and
people in the stream and tide of faith, or are they analysts and
spectators of it? We are sometimes as inept in our effort to do
spiritual work as were those children who brought some birds'
eggs into the house and set them to hatch under an electric
pad! Some of the great churches are waking up to the need for
evangelism. When my own communion, the Episcopal Church,
talks about evangelism, it makes me think of a bachelor, having
married a widow with a baby. She goes out of the house,
leaving the baby on his lap. There the critter is, but he does
not know quite what to do with it. Well, he can learn. So
can we.

The pattern for the local church should be Acts 2:47, "and
the Lord added to the church daily such as should be saved."
The church must have both rebirth and nurture. Some churches
are strong on conversion and weak on nurture: others are strong
on nurture, but weak on conversion. They remind one of
Beatrice Herford's monologue on an English timetable: "O I
see—the trains that start don't get there, and the trains that
get there don't start!" Many churches are carefully shepherding
and trying to train a lot of people who have never begun a
decisive spiritual experience. How can one nurture a plant until

it has taken root? How can one bring up a child that is not born? Of what use is the system of the church, its services and sacraments, its work and its worship, if the hearts of its people are not converted?

The change must begin, I am convinced, in the minister himself. Just a word now "for ministers only." How much time do we give to God in the morning before the day starts? Do we read the Bible to find texts for Sunday, or power for Monday? How well do we hit it off with the wife? Do the children have enough of our time? Are we up against one of the men on the vestry or board of trustees? Do we feel envious when others get bigger jobs and we do not? Are we weighed down with sins unconfessed, hardly even admitted to ourselves? Are we keeping up a brave front in the community, with the church at large, with the church members themselves? And are we really giving people stones for bread, so that we keep them outside the great joy and adventure of Christian practice and faith? Do we need to go to some brother-minister whom we can trust, blurt the whole thing out in tearing but saving honesty, and get straightened out again with ourselves, our people and God? Defeated men talking about vital religion, and trying to organize spiritual campaigns, are not convincing. Most of us ministers need spiritual fellowship worse than any other human thing; a company in which we can let out our souls, be ourselves, stop keeping up an ecclesiastical front, be honest, be childlike, start over again. It is astonishing what one talk with another person can do. The big need comes out, we give it over to God, and God begins to work again—it is as costly and as simple as that!

The failure of most clergy conferences is due to the fact that

the men are talked to death in an overfull schedule, and seldom
have time to let themselves out with one another nor the kind
of leadership which encourages this. If a visitor makes a good
speech, we tend to envy him and want to compete with him;
if he makes a bad one, we are likely to be bored and critical.
We need to coalesce into a spiritual unity which can only come
as we wait in silence on the Holy Spirit together. Most of us
have perfectly adequate doctrinal ideas about the Church, and
its nature and function; but we need yet to *discover* the Church
in action, where the Holy Spirit is evidently present in the
company—present in conviction, present in release, present in
power, present in joy, and present in fruitage! We need a wholly
new kind of clergy conference, where we are not bombarded by
speeches and dried up with plans, but where men get converted
and reconverted through the present power of the Holy Spirit
at work within the company. And all of us should be giving
some time to our brothers in the ministry, sharing with them
our own shortcomings and victories, listening to theirs, and
helping them both in a fellowship and one by one.

A minister without power, and who was seriously considering
returning to a successful business career, came into such a
fellowship. In one parish he saw power that he envied, power
that convicted him. Should he get out of the ministry—or
should he get converted? It is no academic question for many
men. In one communion, of the graduates of one seminary,
27 per cent leave the ministry in ten years; of the graduates of
another, 38 per cent in ten years. Suppose someone had been
there to meet the personal needs of these men in time? Granted
some of them should have gone into other work—how many
were like this man who looked elsewhere because his own heart

was not subdued to God? He began to lose his professional air
and manner—he stopped being ministerial and became a human
being. Soon a talk followed with one of his brethren which got
at the unresolved areas in his life—pride, ambition, unruly
emotions, spiritual ineffectiveness. For twenty years a ministry
of notable spiritual power has been the result. Thousands have
felt the power of his life and ministry. But it all began in him.

Our next immediate responsibility is for our staff. A minister
had a high-powered organist, talented and energetic, whose idea
was that happiness could be found in two places: prominence,
and money. He went after them over all obstacles. A total
individualist, he let no one get near him spiritually. But this
way of living ran its course. His pupils, as well as his choir
members, began to fall away. He came to the conclusion that
he was facing an impossible situation, and resigned. He began
writing for other positions—three hundred letters, no less! But
nothing was forthcoming. His pride was hurt and he was "sunk."
For the first time, the minister could get at him through his
need; for the first time he was willing to listen, and let the
minister say something to him without having so ready an
answer that he countered almost before he heard it. The parson
told him the only thing to do was to turn the situation over to
God—the whole thing, pride, hurt feelings, fear and future—
and let Him work it out for him. This was *absolutely new* to a
man who had been playing in churches for thirty-five years!
They went into church, and knelt together at the altar rail.
They were quiet awhile, then the minister said a prayer, and
then asked him to pray, surrendering his situation and his life
to God. He let go of the problem, so that God might handle it
for him. There the matter now stands. But God is at work in

this fallow time. For he says he always thought before now that Christianity meant to think of all the good things one could do, and then do them. Now he begins to see that faith and self-surrender come first, and that what God does for us is more important than what we do for God.

An Episcopal bishop was confronted with a clergyman within his jurisdiction who is an alcoholic. The man disappeared temporarily from his parish, and the rumor started by his friends was that he was suffering from "aphasia." The bishop said to him, "If you will come clean with me, tell me exactly what happened, join up with Alcoholics Anonymous, and make a clean breast of all this with your people, I will stand behind you." (This bishop speaks not only with episcopal authority, but out of a converted heart which has known and faced his own needs, and therefore believes that other men, too, can be converted.) The clergyman told his vestry the facts, and then the bishop met with them. The man was honest and repentant —what would they do with him? One or two of them uttered a few pious remarks about maintaining "the good name of the church"—as if the church would not have a *far* better name for converting one of its clergy, and giving him another chance, than for throwing him out! The bishop asked whether all of them—the vestrymen—had always done all they should do as Christians, and they allowed that perhaps they hadn't. So they agreed to give the man another chance. A congregational meeting was called and the same procedure gone through. Everything in this was aboveboard, there was no evasion anywhere, the bishop took him to some A.A. meetings. Now he is regularly enrolled and goes steadily, and the man is still the shepherd of his people—a good deal better shepherd, I'll be bound, than if his own chief shepherd had not behaved so much like the Good Shepherd, not only in the challenge he laid down, but in the faith and profound understanding which he showed! How many district superintendents, bishops, moderators, or what-have-you, would have dealt with the situation this way?

Parishes must find conversion, also, in their guilds and societies. Often the aim is lost in detail, and one wonders if a stranger coming in would realize at all that these people meet to serve a great Master, whose presence and power are meant to be the central reality of their lives! We need organizations and guilds, of course, composed of groups of men and women who do a particular job and who take a special responsibility. The quality of their work will be largely determined by the spirituality, or want of it, of their leaders; and it is with them that the minister must work in order to raise the level of it. In one church, the women's association had almost dried up: it was run by old ladies, and the young ones would not come in. One or two spiritually minded middle-aged women came to the conclusion that it should be revitalized. They did not go in with banners flying to "change" everything: they patiently and humbly identified themselves with the best things the old ladies were doing. Slowly, as offices became vacant, they were elected to them. The result is a society with a broader base, wider comprehensiveness, and greater spiritual power, while the old missionary objectives not only have not been lost, but they have been pursued with much greater success.

Clergy, vestries and people are in danger of losing religion when it comes to money. They keep too much for themselves and do not give enough for extension through missions, or they fear to venture in faith where God calls for that, or they run ahead of God's plan and get into unguided debt. But suppose a debt is inherited from the past as happened to one minister? He has a very large church and a very large congregation of quite moderately circumstanced people. He hoped to have the building consecrated on the one hundred and twenty-fifth anniversary date, but the ecclesiastical authority notified him that of course this could not be done until the debt was cleared entirely. It stood at $9,000, and there were six weeks till the anniversary. A snap judgment, either to push it through, or to give it up, might have been made. Instead, the minister gathered a little company of praying men and women, with whom he was in the habit of meeting. It seemed to be the will of God, as they saw it, that the money be raised and the church consecrated. They talked, then, of plans. One made the suggestion that the one hundred and twenty-fifth anniversary gave them their cue: let every person in the parish go out for every fraction or multiple of 125—from $.12½ to $1.25, $12.50 to $125, depending upon the amount individuals or groups might give. The trustees agreed to back the plan. Then on that Sunday morning a great offering of $9,000 was brought in. There were no entertainments, no special efforts, just offerings out of their meager savings or what they had on hand. There are so many instances of God's provision where He has been given the chance to make His will known. It seems that the deficits indicate both want of His guidance, and want of human faith.

Every parish ought to have within it one or more small groups that meet for deepening the spiritual life. A couple that had been brought to a real Christian decision and outlook moved into a suburb and began going to the local church. The husband says, "We felt there should be a fellowship for the parishioners, so that what they learned on Sunday they could talk out together more personally at some other time and see how it could be worked out in their lives. We prayed about it. One day a young man much interested in the church came up to us, and began talking about how some of us might get to know one another better. We told him about such groups, and suggested some of us getting together. So we invited about ten people, of younger married age, to come together and talk about it. Some of them wanted a merely social time, and thought the only thing that would not scare them away was a dance or a card game. But this interested young fellow said he wished they might learn more about the real teachings of the Church. We compromised a little, and we spent the first hour in a discussion of a little book called *The Complete Sayings of Jesus*, then went on into whatever each leader planned. This provided a chance to give what they had, and to bring out questions and concerns which they did not understand. When it came my turn, it happened to be the story of Nicodemus. That gave me the chance to say what had happened to me spiritually. One immature fellow quibbled about being 'born again,' said he thought it just meant being baptized. It led to a real discussion of conversion. One fellow in that group, who is going into the ministry, has come to understand much better the need for a personal relation with God, and for a fellowship in the church."

A church fuss or misunderstanding or division may be the signal for a route—or for a victory. It depends largely on the faith and consecration of the minister. One minister writes, "As you know, last fall I was very low and discouraged. I planned to quit the church and turn it over to someone else. You remember we sat down quietly one day in the church for a while, and then you offered prayer. It was not the first time that I brought my problems to that altar. Again I received help. I began to realize that running a parish is not just like running a business, 'do it my way, or else.' I realized that the first need of reforming was in my own disposition and soul. My wife had for a long time been pointing out that much of the responsibility for the parish trouble was chargeable to me, though it was not entirely my fault. We put our own relation, and our problem, up to God in prayer. In this spirit, we invited some of those who did not think as we did to come to the house for tea and for dinner. We saw individuals, also. I did some pastoral visiting among the older members. By the spring, the spirit of our church was completely transformed. As a material evidence, we had a fine service at which we burned our mortgage and cleared off our debt. (Don't forget four years ago we were completely broke, and the committee had recommended closing us out.) We had a church dinner right after Pentecost, and if ever the spirit of Pentecost was in a church meeting, it was that night. You could feel it in the friendly spirit, and in the exchange of greetings between old and new members. My wife and Mrs. ———— have been going down to the Tuesday prayer group, and have started a similar one in our parish. It is still small, but it will grow."

This badly needs to begin in our seminaries. There are two characteristic sins of theological seminaries: scholarship divorced from life, and deferred realization of spiritual power. It goes without saying that the job of the seminary is to acquaint men with the doctrine, history, sources, worship of the Christian Church. This requires hard intellectual application, and teachers well-versed in their subjects. But seminaries run the same risk as colleges, which is to leave men with no suggestion of a synthesis of what they have learned. Dr. Fosdick says college gave him a lot of spokes, but no hub! Many men graduate from seminaries with plenty of religious spokes —facts, ideas, doctrines, truths; but not so many come out with central hubs of spiritual conviction and experience which they have seen applied to human situations and in which they have already begun to have a share. We need more scholarship of the human heart (and this not only the human heart as found in hospitals and institutions, but out in the pagan and healthy-minded world): we need to teach our theological students to read men, as well as books. And while their attention should not waver from their studies, these studies will be infinitely enriched, and the "word made flesh," as they begin now to participate in cell groups for spiritual growth and prayer, in fellowship with other Christians, and in active evangelism of some kind.

All this, it seems to me, constitutes the next step in the development of the Church—all churches, the Church as a whole throughout the world. We have better organization than ever before. We have more members than ever before. We have access to the best brains in the world, many of them right in our own church leaders. The missionary movement is the most hopeful thing on the horizon of the world, unless it be overtopped by the movement, slow but steady and certain, toward unity. But what we lack, conspicuously and universally, in spite of some encouraging signs, is *great spiritual movement*. One does not look so much for *a* spiritual movement, for this is often associated with a name, a man, a viewpoint, and so soon becomes partial, biased and ineffective. But we do desperately need the movement of the Holy Spirit Himself in and through the churches. Perhaps He is seeding the Church with converted men and women and small cells and companies—it looks as if He might be doing so. But let us not "cease from mental fight," from prayer, from earnest and utter self-dedication to the one end, that the Church of Christ become a "pillar of cloud by day, and a pillar of fire by night" to the people everywhere and all the nations of the earth. This is our greatest need. And God alone can match it with His hour!

CHAPTER V

"By All Means"

GOD broke into the consciousness of the world, as He had never done before, through incarnating Himself in human flesh. He became more real by becoming more concrete. It is always His way. The clothing of the Spirit of God in the flesh of human event is still God's most effective way of making Himself felt and known. The more legitimate ways in which we can let the Spirit of Christ clothe itself today, the more people we can reach. St. Paul says, "I am made all things to all men, that I might by all means save some" (I Corinthians 9:22). What does he mean by this? Certainly not that he shifted his position every time he met a new person, or tried to accommodate His message to fit in with every divergent outlook: in a sense St. Paul was one of the hardest men to budge that history ever saw. But it means he was *adaptable*. He tried to get inside every man, and look out through his eyes. He tried to identify himself with the man's situation, and see how the Gospel would go to work under his particular circumstances. If he could understand people, he could commend the Gospel to them.

Let us explore, then, some of the ways in which we must clothe the Gospel today—we can mention but a few—if we are to become "all things to all men, that we may by all means save some." The phrase "functional Christian living" is full of meat: it seems to mean that each person must live out his faith and make his contribution to it and to the life of the world, along the line of the subject or profession closest to his own heart. Sometimes we ask a man to make too much of a jump, as when we expect a businessman or an artist to function exactly like a minister; and he gets discouraged and feels out of his depth. The movement of the stream of spiritual power seems to be: from God, to the person, through his commitment, to the world.

One "means" that we think too seldom of, is *art*. It is said that we remember about 5 per cent of what we hear, and about 30 per cent of what we see. Has the Church been sufficiently mindful of this? On the whole we are building better churches than we did fifty years ago, but not in all cases; and in some of them the stained glass and woodwork which we permit is little less than barbaric. Is there any way of estimating what Michelangelo has done for man's conception of God by the Sistine painting of Creation? Or what Raphael has done to make the figure of the Christ-child real to us? And who can begin to say what the stained glass in Chartres has done to draw people right up into the Holy of Holies—that majestic, dark interior in which Napoleon said, "An atheist would be ill-at-ease here!" And what have Browning and Sidney Lanier done through words to help people "see the Christ stand," or to "build them a nest on the greatness of God"? And for how many human souls, longing to say the ineffable, have Bach and Beethoven, Horatio Parker and J. B. Dykes, said it for them and lifted up their souls upon the wings of music? If we need one thing in our time in religion, it is more genuine emotion;

and perhaps the surest place to express emotion legitimately and with control is in and through beauty and art. Nearly every artist feels himself the channel of beauty and truth, and his mission must be known and honored. When a professedly pagan organist was asked how he felt, what he really was doing, as he sat on the organ bench and played, he replied quickly, "Giving back beauty to the Author of all beauty." Not so pagan after all! A channel of the beauty that comes from God.

There is Christian witness, also, in the espousal of good and sound causes in community, state and nation. Specific "causes" will arouse disagreement, but light comes as all of us fight for what we believe right. In one small community, a chain store proposed that beer be sold off the premises. This is perhaps the least offensive form of the liquor business; but all know to what it can lead when young people can get liquor anywhere. Some of the people in the local churches, not bluenoses, but responsible parents and citizens, took the time to go before the Alcoholic Beverages Control Board of the state, to oppose the measure. There was no one there to defend it, save the company's lawyer. The opponents, however, took pains not to blacken the name of the company; instead, they said they often traded with that company, and had a high regard for it, and did not wish to see it demean itself by taking this step about off-premises sale of liquor. There is an unchristian way of doing a Christian thing, of which religious people are often guilty. Let us try to do the Christian thing in the Christian fashion, as this group did!

Everyone that is concerned about the religious education of children should see what can be done, not only about church schools on Sunday, but about instruction during the week. The

program of "released time" is best where religious instruction
in the schools is opposed by other religious groups. The New
York State law provides that a child may be dismissed an hour
a week for released time religious instruction, during which
time no advance work is to be given by the regular teachers.
Some teachers get around this by arranging hobby groups at
this time, but released time answers by arranging some hobby
groups of its own! In New York City, ten or eleven thousand
children, a third of the available Protestant children of grades
three through eight, are now enrolled in released time courses.
Where opposing groups are few in a community, the percentage
is as high as 98 per cent. There has come a change in the
attitudes of the children themselves toward it, and they do not
need as much supervision to keep them from running away as
was the case at first. And some of the school principals are
taking a much more positive attitude toward it. When the
mother of one of the released time children died, the child's
public school teacher comforted her and said that she hoped
she could take up her life and face it with courage. The child
replied, "You don't need to worry about me. I go to released
time!"

All who would set forward the Christian interests in a community would do well to identify themselves with the interests
of five groups in the community: the newspapers, the schools,
the radio stations, the moving picture theaters and the book-
stores. Newspaper men, owners of radio stations, and many
others in the community, know all too well the minister or
church member that wants to "use" them for something—to
get in news about the church, or quotes from a sermon, or some
rake-off in charges because the objective is religious: and they

are heartily sick of this approach. How different the approach
of one minister who constantly visits the responsible persons
in all these various strategically important centers, not to grind
his own or religion's ax, but to see if there is any way he can
help them in what they try to do in the community. He has
stopped to help a makeup man with the format of his paper
when he was pressed for time. Such helpfulness incidentally
lead to his having space in the papers sometimes, and spots on
the radio: but these come about quite secondarily. Here again
we are reminded to seek first the kingdom and "all these things
shall be added." Teachers, newspaper writers, moving picture
operators, radio broadcasters and booksellers can greatly color
the thinking of a community—they can be a negative or a
positive influence. Of course, Christian people want to influence
them, but rather for what they can be and do, than for anything we can get out of them. And this may best be done by
genuine helpfulness, making friends, feeling concern for their
problems, and when the right time comes, suggesting a Christian answer and application.

One place where we can all help is in knowing the facts and
standing up for the truth. A well-informed teacher said recently
that nine tenths of the thinking of America is influenced by
left-wing ideas. One of the best answers that has come to the
ideas of Henry Wallace was Norman Thomas' letter to him
after the refusal of Mr. Wallace to debate witht Mr. Thomas
on Russia: he said,[1] "You evade my questions when you pay no
heed to concentration camps with their millions of victims of a
police state as cruel as Hitler's; to the complete lack of civil
liberty in Russia; to the systematic destruction of the little

[1] The New York *Times*, July 6, 1947.

Baltic peoples; to the growing extremes of income between the bureaucrats and workers, extremes greater than in the United States; to the dictatorship's steadfast refusal to enter any kind of co-operation under the Marshall plan or any other device unless under terms consistent with Russian dominance." We should know what is in books like Kravchenko's *I Chose Freedom*, and Christopher Norborg's *Operation Moscow*, and discuss Russia, and international affairs in general, from a Christian viewpoint. If Christianity is not to be and remain an ivory-tower personal privilege, if it is to get down into the realities of the economic and political and social problems of our time, then ordinary Christian people must know how to relate their truth and belief to the general and special problems of the day.

A chance comes to us all every day to lift the level of conversation about human affairs to a higher, more Christian level. Here is part of a letter that describes such an effort: "One night a group of us tried to combat a very materialistic economist who was telling how to solve the world's ills. He thinks there are just too many Indians, Chinese, etc. We should let Europe take care of itself: no use pouring more American dollars in there. We don't even get good will out of it. The best way to help the world is to mind our own business. I said, 'That is not a very Christian solution nor is it a realistic one. If you think we can stay healthy in a sick world, that is not even good economics, let alone sound Christianity.' He tried to brush it off, but I finally said, 'You are advocating just the kind of practice that made two wars. How about Christianity and economics getting together?' "

We can all learn something from the procedure of a Roman

Catholic group which is called the "Convert Makers of America."[2] It aims to "bring Catholic truth to America's millions who are not reached by priest or church. With a nucleus of 800 zealous men and women, most of them converts themselves, the organization" is said to be "rapidly expanding." It has three working divisions: (1) information centers, stocked with explanatory literature staffed by part-time lay "librarians," located in any convenient place with high traffic, as empty stores, sections of offices "and even the front of a beauty parlor"; (2) pamphlet racks, in such places as railway terminals, newsstands, public markets and hotel lobbies. Workers must obtain permission to install the racks and then service them regularly; (3) information talks, to be given at a series of five or six weeks meetings for twelve or fifteen non-Catholics in a Catholic home, with laymen making the talks . . . a parish priest is to 'sit in' on the discussion and answer technical questions. At the end of the series the priest conducts the non-Catholics on a tour of a church, and they are invited to attend Mass during and after the lectures. "Individuals are given simple requests to bring religion into conversation," says the Convert Makers, "with at least one new non-Catholic a month, to invite outsiders to mass, to say a rosary a day if possible for the society and to work actively in one of the three divisions." Each member must choose one "avenue" and must report weekly in a letter upon his activities. This is definite, specific, systematic. Could not most of this plan be lifted right out of its context and be made a basis for Protestant "convert-makers" as well? One hopes that the Protestant-Catholic antithesis is not the main emphasis, but the Christian-Pagan antithesis; for

[2] The New York *Times*, July 13, 1947.

that is where the real axis of irreconcilable difference lies today.

This means that we need pamphlets and books which will both inform and convert people. Our Protestant churches have been stronger, in later generations, on the educational and informative side than on the conversion side. They have failed to remember that nothing will stick in a man's mind which has not already roused and intrigued his emotions. Our Protestant religion has been, on the whole, so intellectual, so theological, so much a matter of ideas and ideals, and so little a matter of warm human interest through our seeing what it does for people, that it has become for many of our Church members a purely academic question which they seek to solve for themselves and for others in a purely academic way. We need a *converting literature* pertinent for today. Why did Harold Begbie's *Twice-Born Men* sell half a million copies? Not alone because Harold Begbie could write; but also because what he said was not in the abstract of religious generalization, but in the concrete of stories about living human beings who had been redeemed. There needs to be more of "experience," more of the natural "before-and-after" presentation of our truth. A story about a person who has found a new life in Christ hooks into the life of so many who hear it: it makes them say, "That's just like me," as the problem unfolds, and when one indicates how the answer came, they make the same application to themselves. People devour books and articles that speak about personal religious experience—and they don't devour big or small general books about the theory of religion. And books which breathe the air of conversion will bring inspiration to many who are far from understanding religion's profound abstractions. Let "the Word be made flesh" in the witness, direct and indirect, of those who say, "One thing I know, that, whereas I was blind, now I see" (St. John 9:25).

Sometimes the Spirit of God is at work when we are almost unconscious of it. Something in one's example or fundamental faith meets a need in another person, and a spark is ignited. A stable, middle-aged church woman went to work temporarily for a man whose life is given to spiritual work with individuals. The experience turned her from conventional church-going to spiritual adventure. She wrote him of that experience, "All unknown to you, while I was doing your correspondence, I was absorbing from it your way of thinking, and the positive, alive, active Christianity you believe in, although we had scarcely any personal conversation. As a result, all my nebulous longings and inner need for something really satisfying from religion were brought into focus. . . . It seems as though curtains have been removed from my eyes and the whole picture of a real, personal, living God is clear. I have such a sense of inner happiness, and trust that the feeling of peace and relaxation will grow. I cannot understand how one can have been a lifelong church member, and have been untouched by this awakening Spirit. My mother was a good Christian, who, I am sure, knew all these things, for she often told us that she had given her life to God when she was sixteen: I knew she was wonderfully good, but felt that her impulse was probably an adolescent emotional outlet. When I now look through her Bible with all of its marked pages, I *know* she had the Truth."

Alcoholics Anonymous are giving a great lead in practical witness to spiritual truth and power, and are often what St. Paul said the law was, a "tutor" to bring people to Christ and

His Church. One must be with these people to feel and know the power of it all—the men and women, some of them still bearing on their faces the marks of defeat and degradation, men and women who have known the depths of loneliness and despair, laughing and talking together, eager for any helpful truth and experience one can bring them. It all grew from the fact that one man saw a change in two other men; he found the same answer himself—then he universalized it with the help of doctors, ministers, psychiatrists and reclaimed alcoholics. There are too few places where one can take a listless, conventional religionist, or a skeptical, unbelieving pagan, and have him "stabbed broad awake" as he will be at an open meeting of A. A. Because the "twelve steps" of their program are so applicable to others than alcoholics, and because there is so much accumulated wisdom about "the cure of souls" in them, they are listed below:

1. We admitted we were powerless over alcohol—that our lives had become unmanageable.

2. Came to believe that a Power greater than ourselves could restore us to sanity.

3. Made a decision to turn our will and our lives over to the care of God as we understood Him.

4. Made a searching and fearless moral inventory of ourselves.

5. Admitted to God, to ourselves and to another human being the exact nature of our wrongs.

6. Were entirely ready to have God remove all these defects of character.

7. Humbly asked Him to remove our shortcomings.

8. Made a list of all persons we had harmed, and became willing to make amends to them all.

9. Made direct amends to such people wherever possible, except when to do so would injure them or others.

10. Continued to take personal inventory and when we were wrong, promptly admitted it.

11. Sought through prayer and meditation to improve our conscious contact with God as we understand Him, praying only for knowledge of His will for us and the power to carry that out.

12. Having had a spiritual experience as a result of these steps, we tried to carry this message to alcoholics and practice these principles in all our affairs.

We must adventure and pioneer in new and fresh ways to make faith live for people. Dr. Francis C. M. Wei, in his lectures on *The Spirit of Chinese Culture*, says that Christianity in China suffers from an insistence on abstractions, a "hands-off" policy as to indigenous tradition, excess of denominationalism, and ritualistic anemia. He suggests as a remedy a "four-center plan," revolving about "Church cells," "Centers of Christian Service," "Christian Seats of Learning," and "Christian centers of pilgrimage." It will be interesting to see what this eminent Christian leader of his people will accomplish in these directions as he returns to China.

The older type of evangelism is obviously out of date. But there will always be efforts to reach people in numbers and in great cities. This account of the Christian Commando Campaign in London comes from a friend who took part in it, the Rev. Jack Winslow: "It was an exhilarating experience to work side by side with Christians of other denominations, and to find with them a deep fellowship in which throughout the ten days no smallest rift appeared. We quickly got together as a team. We worked in complete harmony. And there was rich diversity of talents and experience such as no denomination by itself could have contributed. . . . This must be the norm for all campaigns of this character, *viz.*, campaigns whose objective is to reach the multitude outside the Church. Divided, we are completely inadequate in numbers, in contacts, in intellectual equipment and in spiritual gifts. United, we are a mighty force—how mighty this campaign has shown. We really did reach people at the place of their daily life and occupations. We did not invite them to church. We *went out to them.* That is what the Church today must do. We went to them in factories of every type, both in the lunch hour and when the day's work was over. The welcome varied from place to place, but on the whole it was friendly, sometimes very friendly. The best evidence is that 60 to 90 per cent of these factories invited us for a return visit. Quite often we found allies already there, Christian men and women who came out boldly, in the discussions, on our side. In not a few of these factories there is now a 'cell' of these Christians ready to carry on the work together with the local church workers for whom an entry has now been secured into many places from which they were formerly barred. Some have asked for a permanent chaplain. We also went to a large number of business houses, schools, hospitals and other institutions. Here, too, the reception was in general most warm-hearted; and in these also the Christian leaven is at work, sometimes on a substantial scale. Quite a number of the 'public houses' gave us an excellent hearing. . . . Publicans were friendly, and the men were ready to listen. In one case the publican has invited the local rector to hold a meeting in the pub. every month to answer questions that are always arising about Christianity, and the Church. There is no doubt that the pub. is the place where the parson should often be if he wants to get to know the men of his parish. It is the men's club; and, if he's the right sort, he'll be welcome. Cinema audiences were unexpectedly responsive. . . . The manager would introduce the speaker. Little signs of impatience at the interruption of the programme soon yielded to interest, then to cheers of approval, and at the close of a five or ten minute talk, to a spontaneous outburst of enthusiastic applause. It showed beyond all doubt how ready the average Englishman is today to give a hearing to the Christian message when put across in language people can understand and in close relation to their daily lives . . . all the best in them leaps up in response to one who can show them that for which they are unconsciously longing. . . . Then there was the open-air speaking, in glorious weather, reaching tens of thousands of people daily, penetrating through loud-speakers into their homes. At the Amateur Cup Final between Wimbledon and Leytonstone, at Highbury, the Rev. E. T. Killick, former Middlesex and England cricketer, spoke on Saturday afternoon to the large crowd of spectators. At Twickenham the Commandos were given an hour and a half before and after the match, speaking to a truly vast audience. In the streets, too, the cars with their loud-speakers went around announcing the campaign and giving the message in brief and telling talks. It is pretty certain that the message reached millions in this way. . . ."

There is one "means" that is almost always at our disposal, and that is our behavior and our words spoken to our friends.

There is a girl who works in a great city. She was brought up in the church, and found a vital experience of Christ in the church, which carried her through some difficult personal crises in her life. But it was a very "personal" experience and she never found any other people with whom she could share it. Then one Sunday evening she went to a small meeting where some young people were talking about living faith—faith that does things in the actual world. She learned there were other people who had found a dynamic and vital faith, as she had. She found she was understood when she uncovered a little of her experience. It led to real talks with other people who needed to find faith. The next week she took three other girls herself, and they began finding this same experience. This girl is intelligent, musical, interested in all the things that make life worth while, loves to joke and laugh and have the right kind of fun. But she has become a spiritual spark plug: and where she goes, things begin to happen spiritually.

In her office worked another college graduate, of non-Christian background. She came of a very divided family, and in spite of graduating from a notable eastern college, she was unfit and unready to meet her situation. She had no religious training whatever, no faith, and few of the sanctions in life which faith provides. She went to one of the Sunday evening meetings with her friend. She liked the spirit of it, heard some things she didn't agree with, but decided to go back. And week after week she went. Slowly faith began to come into her heart, by exposure, by contagion, by reason, by reading, and by her own sheer need. One night after the meeting she said to the minister, "May I go into the church for a while?" She went in, and knelt down in the dark by herself. Next day he saw her again and asked how she was. "Fine," she replied, "never had a better day in my life. May I see you soon?" She went to make a real decision to give all of her life that she could to all of God that she understood. Slowly it dawned on her that in Christ all this was summed up, the Christian message is Christ, one's relation to Him fixes and determines all else. Like many of her race, when the decision for Christ is once made a surging love for Him ensues. Everything in her moved her on toward baptism and membership in the church. At once, without any suggestion from without, she began giving generously to the church. And later she felt that she owed so much to Christ that she left her secular job, and went to work in the church fulltime and without pay. How many shorthanded staffs, half-manned mission stations, and overworked ministers and church workers, are paying the price of our *not* reaching people like this, with the message of a Gospel that first brings victory and spiritual abundance into their lives, and then asks for their enlistment in active service? And how many of them wait to hear from someone they know and like, someone with intelligence, sense and natural enthusiasm, about what they believe, what has happened to them, what has brought radiance and wonder into life, and how this can become for them their greatest possession? Truly, the fields are white to the harvest, and the laborers are few. We must shift our gears, come to a new expectation about ourselves and about others, and learn how to be "made all things to all men, that we might *by all means* save some" (I Corinthians 9:22).

CHAPTER VI

The Working "Cell"

THERE is an evident need today for another kind of spiritual gathering than the formal service or the parish organization. Many are finding this need best satisfied in what is often called a spiritual "cell," which is a small, informal company that meets for prayer, or fellowship, or study, or work, or all four together. In many places during the war, such meetings were the only gatherings open to Christians, but all over the world such companies are coming to birth, as if these little groups met a characteristic need of our time. In England there is what is called "The Advisory Group for Christian Cells." These companies are quite numerous and so eager to learn from one another: this group says, "The 'cell' is as old as Christianity. Our Lord called together a little group of twelve . . . St. Paul, too, formed little groups wherever he went."

The meetings of the early Church partook more of the nature of "cells" than of services. A scholar who has made special study of the primitive Christian community, Dr. E. F. Scott, writes: "The Christians were reborn; their natures had undergone a change, so that they now belonged to a new type of humanity. It was only in fellowship with one another that they could rightly live their own individual lives. . . . In the few glimpses we have of them are always together—in prayer, in study of the Scriptures, at the common meal. As in Jesus' lifetime they are not merely a number of persons who believe in Jesus and look for his return, but 'the brethren.' "

Such fellowship grows up out of the nature of man and out of the nature of Christianity. William Temple, late Archbishop of Canterbury, great philosopher as well as great ecclesiastic, said: ". . . the essence of morality is personal fellowship or respect for persons as persons," and "Personality is the capacity for fellowship." And it is evident to any close reading of the New Testament that what we are seeing is not a string of individuals bound to Christ, but a company of men and women bound to Christ and to one another. As Nicodemus says in *Midnight Hour*, "You cannot be a Christian individualist; there is no such thing. You are a member of the Christian community or you are not a Christian in any full sense of the word." As the living Church, then and now, was a fellowship and not only an institution, this means participation in the life of a spiritual movement, and not merely sitting in a pew and being carried along. The "belonging" is not an appendage to Christianity: it is part of the thing itself. It was not ecclesiastical high-handedness nor exclusiveness, but a profound understanding of this essential social and corporate nature of Christianity, which made St. Cyprian, Bishop of Carthage (died A.D. 258) say, "Outside the church there is no salvation."

Modern psychology is moving toward the same conception. A few years ago, psychology considered man in himself, in his emotions, in his reactions, in his conscious and subconscious mind. But today psychology considers man in his relations, and is beginning to say that he cannot be understood, nor can he adequately manage his life, apart from those relations. Dr. C. G. Jung says that "the meeting of two personalities is like the contact of two chemical substances: if there is any reaction, both are transformed." The "we psychology" of Dr. Fritz Kunkel, and the "theory of interpersonal relations" of Dr. Harry Stack Sullivan, are indicative of a trend in psychology that is definitely away from individualism.

The whole world is in search of some principle of free but cohesive community. Perhaps it is the only lasting offset and cure to the tragic and brutal collectivisms which rise up in human life from time to time, proving the wisdom of Dr. John Macmurray's words, "If social unity is not maintained by love, it must be maintained by force, since human life is, in fact, social." We must begin on a compassable and practical scale to find out what community really is, and to create it. Richard Russell says "The rebuilding of Europe cannot now be political; political faiths can no longer move the hearts and spirits of men. . . . The Europe of the future will be built upon these little communities or brotherhoods. . . . The Christian minority can alone rebuild Europe." Interesting confirmation to the effect that, in seeking to build world-wide community we are not begging the question but going right to its solution in building Christian community between persons, comes from a man who tried to do this in a Japanese concentration camp, and who writes, ". . . the power of the constitution, the law or the government of a community is directly proportional to the amount of community responsibility and group feeling that exists there. Coming out of camp, it is interesting to note that many sensible people really feel that a world government can create a world community—in camp we found the cause and effect relationship just reversed; there a declining sense of community responsibility and feeling rendered our constitution and our government almost useless as a force for law and order." And I quote John Macmurray once more: ". . . economic interdependence is not sufficient of itself to create community. For community there is required in addition a sense of personal relationship of which this economic interdependence is the material expression."

Fellowship among Christians has always been one of the best pieces of cement in the whole Christian structure. In it we help one another. The man who is "down" for any reason finds inspiration and lift in what someone else says, who may have been down but has begun to find the way up. This is not, of course, the "Germanic notion of community," which Jacques Maritain says "is built on a nostalgic longing to be together, on the emotional need for communion for its own sake [which] . . . becomes a compensation for an abnormal feeling of loneliness and distress." It is Christian fellowship, the *koinonia* of the New Testament.

Our need for contact with one another was well put in a parable in *The Reader's Digest* of February, 1937. "A certain pastor mourned over a backslider, who had once been a regular attendant in his congregation. He went to the man's home and found him sitting before an open fire. Without saying a word, the minister took up the tongs, lifted a glowing coal from the fire and laid it aside on the hearthstone. In silence they watched it die out, whereupon the backslider exclaimed: 'You needn't say a single word, sir; I'll be there next Sunday!'"

How, then, do these "cells" begin?

A minister on a church staff felt impelled one day to go down into the boiler room to ask the building superintendent if they might have a talk and some prayer together. Something was on his mind and conscience which he felt he should talk over with another human being, and he was led to the superintendent. His honesty provoked honesty in his friend; and they both then took their needs to God in prayer. A bond came between them through this costly but cleansing honesty. They felt they wanted to meet like this again. They agreed it should be once a week. Honesty, fellowship and prayer lifted both men to a new level of victory, and helped keep them there. But this was too good to keep! They invited half a dozen more men in with them—a former pagan who had found Christ and was eager for the fellowship of others in the new life, and a former alcoholic whose faith had saved him from it after thirty years of defeat. These four began meeting regularly. There would be prayer, perhaps some passage of Scripture that had helped one of them especially, catching one another up to date on where they were spiritually and what responsibility they were taking. Others were later included in the meeting. And now that "cell" has been functioning steadily, winter and summer, for six years. Hundreds of men in all walks of life have been to one or more of its meetings, which generally average from fifteen to thirty. Here you will hear men speak of God's power in their own lives, to change them from all manner of wrong and defeat, or of the way Christian principles have worked to transform a business or a home. It began in the simple, costly honesty of two men with each other who let each other know exactly what was and was not happening, and admitted a mutual need for fellowship.

A group of city ministers came to feel that the parochial and denominational approach to their community was not the answer: there must be a united approach. Two of them took responsibility and invited the others one day for lunch. There were as many ideas of how to proceed as there were men present. Some favored another "organization," some a kind of eclectic potpourri of trying to combine all viewpoints. The suggestion was made that the first thing needed was that they know one another as men and as persons, and that for a time the meetings might consist in letting each man in rotation talk freely about himself, his call to the ministry, his emphases, where he felt he was succeeding and where falling down. This broke the ice (and there is often a good deal of "ice" among ministers, what with some denominations thinking themselves superior to others, and some men rating themselves and one another according to the size of their parishes). A fellowship has been formed that has stood through the years. Many new men have been included, the programs have varied immensely; but the original fellowship created among them at the first has persisted. A united service held annually has been an outward sign that all the non-Roman churches of that community are at work together. And when a vast building scheme was put into effect, bringing many thousands of new people into the community, the spiritual opportunity and responsibility which this represented was not dealt with parochially, nor even denominationally. The company doing the building was persuaded to put out a brochure of all the churches and synagogues, and all the special services offered by them, to the new tenants. Names of tenants are given to the interchurch committee, and a visitor has been engaged who will call on them promptly, in the name of all the churches of the community, and then give their names to one of the parishes, according to the people's expressed denominational preference. Such a co-operative venture was the only one that could have won the company's assistance; but it could never have taken place if there had not been the preparation of years of fellowship among the ministers, who have come to know and trust one another and to "bear one another's burdens."

Ralston Young, the Red Cap of Grand Central Station[1] who calls the station his "cathedral," and is forever finding spiritual opportunities to help and serve and witness to his clients, began to feel that there should be some meeting in the Grand Central neighborhood. It was his idea, and two or three white men who worked in offices near by, and whom he had come to know, concurred in it. Why not Ralston as the host? But where could they meet in the swirling human tides of Grand Central Station? Ralston thought of idle cars, standing empty in the yard—there might be better places for a meeting than a day coach, but it would hold quite a few people. He approached the company, and they gave him permission to use a car on track 13. There every Friday noon at 11:55 you will find Ralston and his friends, who will show you to the car. Very soon you will be aware that there is Someone Else in that car beside the brown brother who usually leads the meeting and the other friends who come. The talk is about Him, the fellowship springs from Him, the prayer is addressed to Him. One man with an idea and some faith and some friends. That is how that "cell" began.

Jesus created three groups: the Three (Peter, James and John) with whom He seems to have discussed the affairs of His

[1] See article "My Most Unforgettable Character," *The Reader's Digest*, February, 1946.

kingdom and His mission and who knew Him better than any others; the Twelve, who were the men whom He had called to be His apostles, and who had accepted His challenge and given themselves to His work and to one another; and the Seventy, a special group called out to do a particular piece of missionary work. These three have become a kind of classic pattern. We often find that we need three or four who are our intimates, with whom we can pool all our needs, problems, decisions, joys and sorrows. The best number for a regular "cell" meeting is about twelve: more than that tends to cause people to make speeches, instead of keeping simple and personal, and one can go around the circle of twelve each time, giving each one time to say something, and then let the meeting find a focus in some conviction or plan which comes forth from the company. And again, at a conference, or in the spiritual attack on a city, it will be necessary to call together a larger spiritual force that will find its cohesion largely through the one common objective. Such a company comes together, works, breaks up, and may come together again with some additions and some subtractions at another time for another objective. These "teams" are very essential if we are to move away from the sterile individualism into which so much of Protestantism has degenerated.

Some such companies meet for study and discussion. Dr. William C. Munds, of Christiana Hundred, Delaware, has successfully carried on such groups in his parish for years, and has a third of his members enrolled in them: he is most wise in the amount of leadership he exercises himself, drawing creative leadership from lay people.[2] Some groups meet for

[2] See *Anglican Theological Review*, October, 1947.

prayer and the fellowship of waiting upon God. I have heard
of a group of laymen in New York who meet once a week in a
small company for an hour of united silence: they come and
they go without a word, but they have been together with God
in utter quietness, receptive to His creative working in them,
and trusting to the Spirit, apart from any human words. Some
groups meet to carry out special projects. One group in a city
on the edge of the South met to see what could be done about
better racial understanding: six of them were colored and six
of them were white. Some groups meet in churches, some in
houses, some in offices. Some meet for a series of, say, half a
dozen gatherings. Others strike root and go on meeting weekly,
perhaps for years. One feels that, whatever the basis and
objective may be, there is far more inward growth, and often
far more outward fruitage, from a meeting of about a dozen
people, with enough leadership and leaven to keep the meeting
on the rails, yet with enough freedom and spontaneity for
everyone to make a contribution, raise an objection if there
is one, but at least to participate and therefore to grow and
plan and act, than from the usual spiritual gathering.

In a little Quaker pamphlet, Dr. Elton Trueblood says
some things about cells that are worth quoting: "No civilization
is possible without adventure, and the adventure which our
time demands is adventure in the formation of faith-producing
fellowships. . . . The fellowship must be marked by mutual
affection of the members; by a sense of real equality in spite
of difference of function; by inner peace in the face of the
world's turmoil; and by an almost boisterous joy. . . . A society
of loving souls without self-seeking struggle for personal

prestige or any unreality would be something unutterably precious. A wise person would travel any distance to join it."

What of the conduct of the meetings?

There is usually one leader who because he knows more, or has better qualities of leadership, or started the thing, permanently stands behind it. But he does not lead every meeting: it is his purpose to train as many others as possible to do a good job of leading also. He will not monopolize the meeting, nor make it a forum for his own pet theories, nor crack the whip too much. He will try to evoke the best from everyone, being sensitive to their needs, aware of their victories or defeats, conscious of a new man who needs to be introduced to the company, or of one who has recently had a great experience which will help the rest. The meeting will not be run like a committee: neither will it be too go-as-you-please, for the leader will nicely stop someone who talks too long, turn a controversial subject to one on common ground, draw out the silent, include the shy, and use the spiritually creative.

The meeting may begin with an informal prayer. It may proceed with a brief but relevant exposition of a passage of the Bible. It may be right for one man to tell enough of his own story, or the story of his situation, to give a flavor and set a pace. It is like leaven, and begins permeating the others. Informality, laughter, unself-consciousness, naturalness, honesty, evident practicability—these things make strangers feel at home, and encourage others to say something who may have thought they would feel ill at ease in such a gathering. The life and vitality of the group depend upon the progressive growth and discovery of the men and women who compose it. The progress seems to be: we listen first, then we experiment, then we tell others because it is too good to keep! "We suggest," says Dr. E. Stanley Jones, "that no one argue, no one try to make a case, no one talk abstractly, and no one merely discuss religion, but that we simply share what religion is meaning to us as experienced."

It is an amazing and liberating experience to find oneself in a company where there seems to be no tension, no contrasts, no barriers, no criticalness, and to hear another man say something one might have said himself if one had been honest and unafraid. As the "gathered meeting" proceeds, one will find men talking not above a conversational tone, with the noise of strident voices absent. Thoreau said, "There are many fine things which we cannot say if we have to shout." A restfulness seems to ensue, which is enlivening and not soporific; one often feels more rested after an hour like this than when one came in. In all the neurotic loneliness of our day, think what it does for people to hear others not so much saying these deep spiritual things *to* them, but rather saying these things *for* them, as if a truly led person were uttering what is in the hearts and minds of all, needing only to be uttered to bind them into a God-given unity. Crucibles of experience, centers of inspiration, builders of fellowship, these companies are drawing many into faith today and showing them how to increase it, and how to put it to work.

Here are ten suggestions about "cells" from one who has been conspicuously successful in helping others to create them, the Rev. W. Irving Harris:

1. Nothing happens while we merely think about starting a cell, so pray for God's direction and *try* something. Everyone

makes mistakes, but he who wants to be used will find both like-minded people and a practicable plan.

2. Keep the group *small*. If you must enlarge, then form a "heart-beat" out of those three or four who are most spiritually in earnest and meet with them for prayer and planning at a different time from the larger meeting.

3. Accent *friendliness*—it is a sign of love. It is emotional release which leads people to say what they think and "this will be created largely by the leader's hospitality to them and their ideas."

4. Keep the room, whether in home, church, or office, coolly ventilated and eliminate glaring lights and unnecessary noise. Avoid using a table.

5. Welcome *silences*—they can lead to conviction and conversion when used patiently, without fear or embarrassment.

6. A silence closed with the Lord's Prayer helps a cell to gain unity and strength and leads individuals to rediscover their voices.

7. *Draw out* those who are moving forward spiritually, or have just made a decision of some kind, and let the meeting take flavor from them. If debates arise, suggest that those who are in disagreement talk through the points at issue privately at another time. Relate examples of God's power at work; tell how you first came to know Christ yourself. Give illustrations of helping other people and bringing Christ's Spirit to bear on business and community affairs.

8. Use the Bible when you find a story which relates to the life of the cell or the outreach of that life in the community and world.

9. Keep the separate meetings *short* and stop on time. Those

who want to linger can do so, but some must leave promptly
and you will not get these back if you are indisciplined in
closing.

10. *Follow up* all meetings by talks with one or more friends
individually. Get the habit of praying aloud with one other
person. In your own devotions, ask God to show you what to
do next for "A" or what further step to suggest to "B." Think
of those who come as you think of your children, and ask vision
for them.

God seems to have His own "economy" in dealing with His
world. At different times He uses different instruments. Time
was when the great evangelistic instrument seemed to be great
meetings with a great speaker. John Wesley began his mighty
work in this way, though he conserved it in "class meetings"
which were the right kind of "cells" for that time; it was a bad
day for Methodism when these were dropped, instead of being
adapted better for our own time. Much foolish and prejudiced
talk speaks of great evangelistic meetings as if they were always
emotional and ephemeral; but there are thousands of living
men and women who owe their first faith in God to men like
D. L. Moody and "Billy" Sunday. However, that method does
not seem to be the characteristic method for our day. And while
personal, man-to-man work must ever be the foundational work
of evangelism, the "cell" is perhaps the characteristic instrument which God's Holy Spirit is using today.

There is a profound *psychological* reason for this at this
particular time. People today are, on a very wide scale,
"neurotic" and self-centered. Their answer will be found, not
only in faith in God, but in fellowship with people: they will
find themselves, and begin to be themselves, when they find

open, warm, satisfying relations with even a few people. Only a Christian group will give them deep fellowship without trying in some way to "use" them: the totalitarians of all varieties know well the strategy of the "cell" and use it for evil ends. There is also a profound *social* reason for the emergence of cells today. We seek now, not only Christian persons, but Christian relationships, knowing that only as persons live out their lives into other lives do they truly live at all. The world is filled with social tensions—racial, class, economic, political, national. The sight of one bridge built between individuals naturally on opposite sides of the stream, between two men who meet democratically as Christians, and are not divided by any other belief or condition whatever, is more than welcome—it is hopeful, it may offer the beginning of a solution. A brilliant Negro teacher found himself in a "cell" with a varied company of men—Catholics, Protestants, ex-Jews, Negroes, businessmen, lawyers, architects, missionaries, ministers, teachers. He listened for a time to what was said, and was evidently more interested in the way these men got on with one another, and in their possessing a common ground, than in the fact that each of them individually had found God. Before he left he said, "I am not a Christian. My father is a minister, but I have reacted against the church and all that. But I do want to say that, if what I have heard here today, coming from such a diverse company of men, is true, then Christianity may offer us the basis of human solidarity for which we are all looking." This indicates the larger social significance of spiritual "cells."

William James once said, "The bigger the unit you deal with, the hollower, the more brutal, the more mendacious, is the life displayed." In these days when the totalitarianisms are proving with hideous certainty the truth that is in his statement, we must counter with the building of Christian community. We want this to touch, not alone human relations, but all human institutions, making and keeping them "human," personal, democratic. But it must begin with Christianized relationships. Men must discover that they can live on a basis of fellowship with men whom they *have* seen (in a cell), in order to learn that they might live on a basis of fellowship with men whom they have *not* seen (in a great institution). Here the leaven of Christianity works not alone in human hearts, but in the relations between persons. Here the return to health and sanity and soundness and happiness of our split and sickly and uneasy society must begin to come. And here is a place where all can have a part, and all can take responsibility.

CHAPTER VII

Some Spiritual Principles

THE important factor in effective spiritual work with people is, of course, the part which the Spirit of God plays, working in and through us upon them. We must pray before, during and after our contact with them, whether this be public or private. The special understanding and power that God gives in one address or interview is a new thing in the universe, a little different from anything that ever happened before. This original and spontaneous quality is often the channel of power, and is due to our openness toward God, and toward those we seek to touch, through there being no emotional stoppages in us, and to the fresh working of the Holy Spirit at this hour.

This does not mean, however, that there are not some fixtures of a moral and spiritual nature which should govern our work, some principles of which we must be aware, a framework within which God works through us into the lives of others. We shall touch upon a few of these now.

What general principles govern our knowing the will of God through receiving His guidance? A young man tells me he listens to God, but never hears anything. Why? Perhaps he already knows something that God wants him to do, but has not done it—maybe a simple, mundane thing like paying a bill, or putting his room in order, or writing a letter. Perhaps he is seeking God's guidance to help him with a plan, even a life plan, which he has conceived but which he has not submitted to God for His approval. Perhaps he is out of the stream of God's will, and wants to know God's mind about some one issue, when he does not want to give over his entire life to God and do His will in everything. Perhaps some definite wrong is holding him in one area of his life, and he does not want to let go of it. To have the guidance of God, we must want to do the will of God—all of it that we know, all of it that we can know, no matter what it is or where it leads. Again, one can try too hard to listen to God, and cut the flow of His guidance. We ought to seek first, not guidance, but God—otherwise we run the risk of trying to "use" God for ourselves. Of course, it is not a "voice" that we hear in any audible way: rather, when we expose our minds to God, like a film exposed to light, an impression is created. It is perhaps impossible to determine where our thoughts stop and God's begin; it is not so very important—the important thing is that our minds are free and yielded enough to "think His thoughts after Him." As we wait on Him, regularly, often, with sufficient time, about everything, a course of action is often indicated, a way clears, we know what we should do. "The secret of the Lord is with them that fear (i.e., reverence) him" (Psalm 25:14). And Rufus Moseley has a wise word for us here: "The nearer the Guide, the better the guidance."

How does one make a decision? Gather all the facts—inspiration never yet was a substitute for hard intellectual work. "Talk to wise people," as Henry Drummond advised, "but do not regard their decision as final." Let others who spiritually understand you well know what confronts you, and ask them to pray for you and maybe with you about it. Be sure your mind is rid of overwhelming feelings toward or against a certain course, that the whole situation is yielded wholly to God. Pray about it as you do other things, so that you get the implications of a decision in relation to the rest of your life. Either there will come a flash of direction, or a steady settling of the will one way or the other. The most important factor in making a decision is opening the whole situation up to God, and to another human being, or a group of them. Let those who know you best help you to see the way your natural bias can pull you one way or the other. When you have done all you can to find light, make the decision and go ahead fearlessly.

One who is to do the kind of work indicated in this book needs adequate spiritual intake. If he is to help people he must be mentally awake and alert and this means reading and studying. He must keep physically well, as we shall point out in a moment. Above all, he needs spiritual nourishment and enrichment. He will find it partly in the fellowship of others who are seeking to do the same thing, as indicated in the last chapter. He will find it partly in common worship with the great body of other Christians. He will find it principally as he uses *every available moment for prayer*. Let the mind relax its grip upon an immediate task, and it should fly upward to God instantaneously for a fresh draught of light and power. Pray for what has just been done, or what is next to be done. Saturate your life and outlook in prayer. "Withdrawal and return" are the words which Arnold J. Toynbee uses in his monumental *A Study of History* to describe the periods when the mystic or creative personality goes apart for further inspiration, and then comes back to the crowd with what he has been given. The secret of the loss of power in the lives of many religious workers lies in their insufficiency of prayer.

What should govern us about the getting and spending of money? Many great Christians and Christian movements have lived by "faith and prayer," making no appeals and no sly references to their needs: and God has honored them. Others make frank appeals for their work and so compete with secular needs. We should not, I believe, ask for more than we need; and if we ask in faith, it is my experience that God will give us what we need, though not always what we want or *think* we need. There is enough in this world for everybody's need, but not enough for everybody's greed. Sometimes we come up against a decision: shall we build a big church, and go into debt? Where does faith stop, and foolhardiness begin? We must get to the motive: do we want the glory of a big building, or is it really needed? Huge churches with mortgages on them are poor witnesses to Christ. Better wait until more is in sight before we build, and be sure we are not running ahead of God. God is constantly putting us out on a limb, where but for His help we should find ourselves in trouble: we should not put ourselves out on a limb by human overreaching and ambition. The only people who seem to be doing all they should for the church are the "tithers" who give 10 per cent of their income to God and the Church. Only by the increase in such givers shall we adequately care for the maintenance and extension of the church's work. This is not going to be accomplished by greater pressure on them to give, but by deeper conversion in their own hearts.

Nowhere are we more likely to make a mistake than in dealing with individuals who ask for money. We often give it to them (1) because we have been mean, and want to break the habit, or (2) because we are generous, and like the reputation for it, or (3) because it is the easiest way out of the situation. There is not money enough in our parish budgets to give to all the people who ask for help as much as they want us to give them. Where we know sick, aged, dependable people, or those in temporary distress, money may be wisely given. But the casuals, the "sharpers," the alcoholics, the plungers with a wonderful scheme—we shall waste a lot of God's good money if we do not know how to deal with them. The thing to deal with is not their immediate distress, but their fundamental needs, what lies behind their present predicament. Often one finds a pattern of shiftlessness, dependence, irresponsibility. If we want to help them, really and permanently, let us deal frankly with these, and not play Providence to them with money God has entrusted to us to spend wisely for Him.

It will often be easy to wear ourselves out physically working for others, unless we make careful provision for enough rest and sleep, the right diet, and regular exercise. People are the most fascinating, and the most exhausting preoccupation in the world! When we go to bed let us pray for the ability to leave behind the problems they have brought through the day: let us pull down a curtain in our minds, after we have prayed for them and committed them to God. That is all we can do. Our Lord never worried where He could not help. We should make our bodies, like our minds, good and serviceable machines which we use for the accomplishment of our God-given destiny and purpose in the world. Tired, jumpy, stringy, nervy parsons and church workers and Christians generally are a very poor advertisement. If we work without worry, we shall reach a healthy fatigue at the end of the day; but we should, in general, be able to make up in a night for the energy we have burned up in a day. Some parsons take Saturdays off, not Mondays; it is not only better to think of something you might say tomorrow, than of something you wish you had said yesterday; but we owe it to our people to appear in church rested and vigorous, able to give to them of energy and health, as well as of concern and the Grace of God. Dr. Alexander Whyte, the famous minister of Free St. George's, Edinburgh, used to say: "Squander your life, but be careful of your health."

Nowhere do we need fixed principles more than in our human dealings. Let us consider a few of them.

Deal always in the truth. The truth is the salt of sound human relations, as love is their sweetness. We need both at all times. When a relationship is all love, and no truth, it becomes squashy and sentimental, and the health goes out of it. A whole family is neurotic, selfish, impossible, because a man has always indulged his wife. He calls it love, but nobody else would call it that. Many sentimentally religious people prefer the soft and easy ways of love to the difficult and challenging ways of truth. If nations are to find and keep peace, they must go back of their interests, back of the patriotism of their people, to justice based on law. If people are to find and keep peace, they must go back of their desires, and the support of their well-wishers, to the truth as it really is. This truth must come out: it is germane to the situation. If we fear to speak it, we shall go round in circles and get nowhere. "The truth shall make you free"—the whole truth, and nothing but the truth. Not one side of it, not the truth that supports your side, but the truth as it really is.

Part of the truth always includes our own shortcomings. We do well to begin by confessing them. When I confess my own sins, I tend to make peace, and when I confess the other person's sins, I tend to make war. You may have to say a very strong word to someone about something he has done that is wrong; begin by saying you have done something at least analogous yourself. Someone has said, "If you point a finger at another, there are three fingers pointing at yourself." A Chinese proverb goes, "Peace does not say, I am right." If we will begin with what is wrong in us, the other person will generally follow suit with what is wrong in him; and even if he doesn't, our honesty has given us both a right and an opportunity to ask a like honesty of him. It is this which Christ means by "turning the other cheek"—expose yourself to the other person by frank admission of where you have fallen down. It will take the wind out of his sails, when he thinks you are coming to criticize him, if you will first criticize yourself. Our ability to be just and fair, to keep facing all facts, is bound to win out in the end, even if the end is far off.

Speak the truth in love. Most of us speak flattery in love, and we speak the truth in resentment. We use truth to fortify and justify our own position, to defend ourselves rather than to seek a real solution. There should be no anger in our eyes or voice as we say it; we need to get our "righteous indignation" dealt with before we come face to face with the person. The righteous indignation may be well deserved, the facts may warrant it; we ought to hate evil, in others as well as in ourselves. But blazing eyes, raised voices and angry words usually make matters worse, whereas an attitude of undiscourageable good will, hopefulness and faith will make them better. If temper gets away with us for a moment, apologize for it quickly; the whole incident may set us forward if we do not give in to the pride of excusing our tempers! We are not out to get our own way, or win our own point; we ought to be out to change the person and the situation. If we have bathed it all in prayer before we come to talk about it, we shall find God has come there before us, and a miracle is ready to begin, if it has not already begun.

Speak the truth to the person concerned—not to anyone else. The amount of mischief that has been increased by gossip— some of it the gossip of people in the Christian Church—is unlimited. We love to go with the tale of another's wrong, and be the first to tell so-and-so! Such talk is like spreading germs. Not alone does it increase the wrong by increasing the knowledge of it, but it will usually unfit us ever to do anything constructive about the person of whom we have gossiped. We may hear of a wrong through the gossip of another; take that fact in confidence, lay it before God, pray, and do what He says. But *never* divulge that to another, except where morally you do not see what should be done, and you go to some well-trained and mature Christian and lay the situation before him, anonymously and in confidence, and ask his advice. There is always some temptation when one is the recipient of many confidences to show how much one is trusted by letting some of the confidences slip out: one does not quite mean to do this—sometimes one simply has a leaky tongue. Pray to God to stop the leak, or you will never be fit to be entrusted with the confidences of other people.

Take responsibility, not sides. Hardly a conversation will take place in which one does not hear of some conflict with another. Listen interestedly, and draw out the facts. Though the teller might be injured innocence itself, do not take sides. There is another to be heard, also, and only as one knows both sides, and is trusted by both, can he bring the truth that will set the relationship on the right basis. We must watch and control our emotions, or they will betray us. We need enough sympathy to hear the story out, enough objectivity to hear some of the things the other person is saying *in absentia*. We may heal it all by helping the person before us to go to the other party with an honest admission of where he has been wrong, which may start the solution of the situation. Or we may need to see and hear both sides. Our capacity for objective judgment, for suspending judgment, for helping the individuals concerned to make up their own quarrel, is the measure of our maturity, and our capacity to realize how much more important it is to act wisely than it is just to sympathize or "emote" all over the place.

Don't let people down. A counselor may have put up a stiff challenge to someone, and he is smarting under an acute conviction of sin. He wants sympathy and an easy way out. He will try to get it from another counselor. A man died in his sins because, after the challenging advice of one counselor, who told him frankly his relations at home were utterly self-centered and wrong and needed to be changed, the man called in his minister, who buttered him and flattered him, and told him the other counselor was too stern and should not have spoken to him that way! I do not know what the sin against the Holy Ghost is, but I think this is one of the sins: when a man has been used by the Holy Ghost to bring genuine conviction of sin in the life of another, and a third comes in who lets the whole situation down. Sometimes at a religious conference, after a challenge, you will hear two or more persons in a huddle, criticizing or making fun of what was said: it is a "let-down party" in full swing! Let us honor the work of the Spirit who "shall convict the world of sin" by doing nothing to prevent the often surgical work with which He begins His dealings with the sons of men.

Don't fear opposition. The Christian message has always converted some, and convicted others. It still does the same thing. Someone said that wherever St. Paul went he had a riot or a revival. He generally had both. Nobody need fight the milk-and-water pap that is sometimes passed out as religion: it has neither blood nor bones, and is hardly the ghost of Christianity. But the real thing gets under people's skins, makes them uneasy till they do something about it, and meantime often makes them very hard to get along with. They may for a time have a knife out for the fellow God used to bring this conviction to them. One reason why some of our churches have never got a real plan of evangelism going is that they are trying to find something that will please everybody—the half-converted and hypocritical within the fold, and the pleasant pagans on the outside—and there just isn't any such commodity. If the Gospel begins moving in power, you will always get opposition, from individuals under conviction, or from interests that are challenged about the social value of their product or their practice. We must be as loving as we can, and try not to meet them with anger and fight fire with fire. But we shall be foolish if we expect to do the kind of work outlined in this book and be universally popular for it!

Another most important spiritual principle is *restitution*. It is seldom possible for a human being to do wrong without hurting someone else. Very often its chief evil consists in the harm it has done to others. How do we deal with this? Some counselors are content to help the person to *see* it, and understand the principle. Some spiritual advisers will merely lay upon such people a light penance. Whatever this may do for the soul of the immediate person concerned, it leaves the relationship broken. The matter is not mended until the penitent person goes to the wronged person, admits his own share in the wrong, and does what he can to right it. We cannot atone for our sins: only Christ can do that. But we can make restitution for them in many cases. Nothing but this gets at the pride which is almost always deeper than the immediate cause of the sin—e.g., temper, greed, jealousy, impurity, fear, etc. A highly respectable church woman realized in middle life she had never really been converted. A conviction of sin came to her one Sunday morning at Holy Communion. She recalled years ago having taken some money from the till of a library where she was working, and not having returned it. What should she do? She was well known in the place, and it was small—she would send it back, with accrued interest of course, anonymously! Her minister was consulted as to whether this was sufficient, and he said, "Let us ask God if it is what He wants." They prayed. A conviction came to her that she must return the money *over her own signature*, and that anything else or less was moral cowardice. It was a great step ahead for her, and launched her in the full stream of spiritual faith and discovery, whereas she had been but wading in its shallows before. We do people a great disservice when we do not hold them to such costly restitution as clears their relationships, as well as their souls.

Perhaps the most difficult principle for most ministers and church folk to learn is the *need for fellowship and a team*. A few trusted men who increasingly know one intimately—one's talents and foibles, gifts and biases—can be of inestimable help in our spiritual growth. Most people think they grow just automatically, like a plant in the ground. But we actually grow *by decisions*, by meeting new situations, facing and accepting new challenges, using new muscles. A church service a week, a job to be done for the church, even attendance at a Christian "cell" meeting, may not be enough. Why is a certain parson unable to keep a secretary? Why does another drink too much? Why does another barricade himself behind secretaries and doors? Why do hundreds of them feel lonely, unable to talk to anyone, frustrated, till they slink off and consult a psychiatrist? It is because they lack the fellowship of a team. Pray for such a team. Draw upon men who will stand up to you, not stand in awe of you. It will multiply any man's spiritual effectiveness many times over, and it will provide for him a spiritual checkup which otherwise he may never have. Most ministers are entirely too much "the parson"—the person —in their parishes. The final word is inevitably theirs about most spiritual questions: all the more important, then, that that word be as wise, as considered, as relevant, as God-guided, as possible, and hence the need for a small and trusted company with whom open, frank relations can be fully enjoyed. How can a man be expert in community, as a minister is meant to be, when he does not pursue community himself on a regular basis with a few people? This takes time, and it is often harder on our pride than on our schedule: but it saves time in the end.

The last principle to be considered is this: keep preoccupied with individuals. It is not the main job of the church to turn out a lot of work, list a long string of members, or raise a lot of money: it is the main job of the church to fashion people who behave like Jesus Christ. They cannot be hewn out of the mediocre mass wholesale, but only one by one. We need an organized framework for effective evangelism, as we need an effective framework for our parish work: these are like the steel structure of a building. But how many have become so preoccupied with their means that they have forgotten their ends? Santayana once defined a fanatic as a man who redoubles his efforts when he has forgotten his aims. If this kind of effective spiritual dealing with individuals, outside and inside the church, can only be done by scrapping some organization, let it go! Many parishes are overloaded with them now. Rufus Moseley says that if one has plenty of gas and power, a Packard is preferable to an Austin: but if one has got to push it, an Austin is better! Certain parishes should be stripped down to miniature organization and thus afford ministers and laymen the opportunity to learn the great spiritual art of winning and training others. It seems an almost universal experience that unless one puts this kind of work first in his life, it will be crowded out entirely. Our minds, our emotions, the hours of our day, should be filled with a special group of individuals at all times—individuals we seek to win, individuals we seek to train in taking responsibility, individuals to whom we look ourselves for spiritual fellowship and help. A man's ministry should not be centered in ideas and in organizations; it should be centered in the Holy Spirit and in people. So far as it is humanly possible, we should seek to be open to every human being that wants to see us about the deeper things, though we should have a growing team of trained folk who can help us with them when the load gets too heavy, as it will if one learns the great secret of fishing for men. When parish organizations are filled with converted people, the work will get done, but it will be done in a Christian way, making Christians as it proceeds.

CHAPTER VIII

"Beginning With Me"

ONE hopes that a conviction is everywhere growing that unless there is spiritual awakening on a large scale, mankind may be doomed; and that unless this awakening begins in the Church, it will never reach the world. People like us make a Church like ours, and a Church like ours fails a world like ours. It will be of no avail to see these things unless we act upon them. Bishop Lawrence used to say that the great American heresy is to think that because a thing has been *said*, it has been *done*. So far we have only said it—said it inadequately, but tried to come to grips with the facts and the truth. So many books are written to stir us up, and we get such shallow impressions from them that by and large we go on to our old way and nothing is different. Perhaps we have come far enough to be saying to ourselves: "We don't want to do that this time. We love Christ and know Him to be man's only Saviour and Hope. We do not want to fail Him. He has left His cause in the fallible hands of such as we are. It all comes back to us. Unless we go up on a higher level, reach a greater spiritual expectation and effectiveness, and learn to transmit faith to others, there is no one else to do it."

Of course, the reaction of some may still be that they simply cannot do this firsthand, man-to-man spiritual work. It was step enough for them when they took on a little committee work in the church, or some financial canvassing: but more they cannot undertake. We turn over the old excuses in our minds: we are shy and do not like to wear our hearts on our shirt sleeves. Religion is such a personal thing—what right have we to try to foist it on anybody else? Who are we to be doing this kind of thing? We'd never find the right person, or the right time, or say the right word. And yet—we remember that if all Christians down the ages had given in to this false humility, instead of going forward in the true humility of trusting God to use them as they offered themselves to Him, Christianity would never have progressed and girdled the earth. We should be still in our darkness. We remember that Jesus and the apostles both lived *and* talked—what they said came out of what they believed, were and did. They put spiritual truth and experience into immortal words which have been to us and to millions the carriers of the Gospel. As for us, we cannot forever teeter between the conviction that we should be doing direct spiritual work, and making excuses for ourselves when we do not.

Let us go more deeply into our own souls. If we were completely honest, should we not have to say that it is not shyness and self-consciousness that are keeping us from doing this kind of work, but vagueness and indecisiveness of experience, lack of anything specific that has ever happened to us, to which we can give witness? William James said that religion is either a dull habit, or an acute fever. For how many of us in the Church is it a dull habit? Do we really want a great transforming experience to come to us? "Are we hoping that something may happen?" writes Karl Barth, "Are we not rather hoping by our very activity to conceal in the most subtle way the fact that the critical event that ought to happen has not yet done so and probably never will? Are we not, with our religious righteousness, acting 'as if'—in order not to have to deal with reality?"

What is "the event that ought to happen"? Is it not the wholehearted commitment of ourselves to Christ, way down in the deep places of us, the forsaking of our cherished sins, the discipline of our lazy bodies and minds, the fashioning of ourselves for one great end: to be His servants and His instruments? The Church is full of people whose commitment to Christ is safe and limited. If it were true that the ego had been brought up under the Cross, and nailed there with Christ, we should come away with our hearts on fire, and our faces shining, and our lips only too ready to make known the wonders of His grace. Dean Inge says, "It is our personal defects that hamper us: our mental sluggishness and our want of sympathy; yes, and the heavy burdens which we have to carry, in the sins which do most easily beset us." If once we truly let go, God could use us—all of us. Water can run through any kind of pipe—copper, lead, tin, wood, gold—if it is only open.

Gamaliel Bradford writes, "The true religious idealist, the true purveyor of the gospel, no sooner receives the light himself than he is seized with this passion for distributing it. As we see, for example in Moody, or in Booth, the instantaneous result of conversion is the impulse to convert others, to share as widely as possible the greatest joy and benefit that this world or any other has to give." What does this mean? If we have not the "impulse" to give to others the faith which is the greatest blessing of our lives, is there not a question whether we have ourselves truly "received the light" in more than a fractional form? Some of us got under the wire, and joined the church, on pretty flimsy conviction and a slim amount of experience. We thought we would grow, and that the church would itself provide opportunities for this; but maybe the church has bogged down into mediocrity, lost its high sense of expectation, and become content with people who come to services and pay their promised amounts. The church is far too often more concerned with *pews* and *dues* than with *news*.

Stanley High, a roving editor of *The Reader's Digest*, recently challenged the church for not challenging him: "I think that the first business of the church is to redeem me. And I don't mean to redeem me in the merely social sense which convinces me that the Golden Rule ought to be my Confession of Faith. By redeeming me, I mean personal redemption—the process by which I'm spiritually shaken apart and spiritually put together again, and from which I—the personal I—emerge a totally different person. . . . The first reason for this failure is that the church—the modern, modernist Protestant church—rates me altogether too highly. It has been one of the glories of Protestantism that it has put its emphasis on the Individual, on Free Will and Free Choice. But the net result may prove to be disastrous. . . . I'm simply not as good as modern Protestantism assumes me to be. I haven't got the spiritual stuff to do, on my own, what modern Protestantism expects me to do. The church has failed because it has given me too much freedom and too little discipline. . . . It has assumed that all I needed was the right hand of fellowship, when . . . what I am in greater need of is a kick in the pants. . . ."

The greatest need in the Church is for *just that*. Who will challenge clergy, bishops, eminent and loyal laymen? If the difference between the greatness of the need of the world, and the smallness of our ability to meet it, even with the most potent and priceless possession on earth in our hands—if this does not challenge them, what likelihood is there that anything else will? Most of us who call ourselves Christians need a radical, up-to-date overhauling. A thousand small compromises or hidden defeats have crept in till we are bound, as with many tiny strands, and cannot get free. If our neuroses or conflicts grew serious enough, we should probably seek out a good psychiatrist. He would try to get to the bottom of our trouble by asking pointed questions, and if we gave him truthful answers he might be able to point out the root of our difficulty. But no man can help another who wishes half to reveal, and half to conceal, the truth. All parsons should be trained in the spiritual art, and be able to help one another in these deep places of need. If we Christians were ourselves victorious, we should be doing it all the time, and the level of the Church would steadily be raised. We need, most of us, some drastic, intimate dealing on the part of someone with understanding and sympathy, but someone also with utter honesty who has himself paid the cost of moral and spiritual victory. Unless men have done this, they will be—far from doers of this kind of work—its mortal enemies, and they will fight it in a hundred disguised ways. Many a parish or community awakening was murdered at birth by some nominally religious man who covered his personal defeats and consequent animosity to all challenge, with learned phrases and smart evasions. It has not been paganism without, so much as defeat within, the Church that has prevented awakening. Most of us will never get at that pride which underlies all our other sins, until we go to some other human being, and make a clean breast of our condition. To face that pride with a view to unhorsing it permanently is perhaps impossible, except as we find another who himself knows the Christian secret, and talk with him in the light of an already realized Higher Power and at least the dim awareness of the forgiveness which alone can come from Atonement.

But a human agent can go only so far. He must finally usher us anew into the Great Presence, and leave us there with our Lord Himself. Our greatest and deepest need is for a greater awareness of Jesus Himself. We shall approach this as we realize that the true initiative is on His side, not ours: we are not seeking Him, as if He were a thing to search after, but He is seeking us, as we are like lost sheep. So many of us, anxious with the weight of the world on our shoulders, or our personal misfortunes absorbing all our emotion, want somehow to *use* Christ, His religion, His Church, to give that comfort to ourselves, and that peace to the world, which will ease the tension. We must get all this turned around the right way. He is the world's Maker and Saviour. He redeemed us with His Blood. He wants the knowledge of that redemption extended by His growing Kingdom throughout the whole wide world. Before we seek to grow too busy helping Him to extend His redemption, let us come back and *rest in it ourselves* for a while. Let the greatness of His salvation stir our minds, its mercy steal down into the crannies of our hearts, till we are

overwhelmed with it. We cannot find the Answer, we can only
be found by the Answer. Do we really trust Him to do with
us and our world what ought to be done, provided we are
obedient to all the light we have, and so do our part?

A woman said a very wise word not long ago. For the
first time she was compelled to do her own cooking, and she
said, "I rather dreaded it, until I discovered how much the
fire does." Have we learned how little is our part, in com-
parison with the other mighty forces, physical and spiritual,
with which we co-operate? Have we learned that we do not
go on our own power, nor in our own light, but in that which
comes from Him who is the world's Light because the fire of
the Father's love burns undimmed and undiminished in Him?
Let us stop a moment, and let Him come into us anew, renew
His grip upon us, His connection with us, His power and grace
in our hearts. . . . And then let us remember that it is this divine
flow which we have just experienced that is the one thing for
which this world, above all other things, is waiting.

Christ comes to us with the gift of moral clarity. He lifts us
up out of that moral chaos and fog which is the world around
about us. We shall come to a new kind of hatred of evil,
wherever it may be entrenched, in ourselves, or in others, or in
institutions. As I write, I am looking out my study window
at a little job I did this summer. The grass had grown out
over the edges of a macadam road, till one could not tell where
the grass stopped and the road began. With a little digging, I
found where the edge was meant to be, stretched a taut line,
cleared out the grass, and set in a small brick wall. Now it
is clear where the grass stops, and the road begins! It is Christ
Himself who comes to straighten our edges, to draw the taut

line that divides what belongs to Him from what belongs to the old self. "The old must be done away," says that wise old Quaker Isaac Penington, "truly done away, and the new come in the place, so that flesh and self may be quite destroyed, and nothing but Christ found in you, and you found nowhere but in Christ."

He will give, too, a new passion of prayer. Prayer is the living communication between Him and us—surrender on a sustained and current basis. It is simple to run up a tentacle of your mind into the heavens, like the aerial on your car, letting intercession run up it, and messages from Him come down it. Some prayer is so small, anxious and selfish; but some prayer is so large, trustful and powerful when we are fully in the stream of God's will. Our lives need simply to be drenched in it. Our touch and service and talks with people should be, also. When we have truly prayed, it is as if the work were already half done when we begin it. People should walk through our prayers in droves. Sometime try the experiment of a continuous chain of intercession, letting those whom you know pass before your mind as one suggests another, and praying for each as they pass. Pray for other pray-ers who will join you in that multiplied power that comes when "two of you are agreed as touching anything." Prayer releases the gifts of fresh grace upon us hour by hour. In it we participate in the creative and redemptive work of God. We need to pray at regular periods in the day, but we need to pray also at every free moment.

And it seems to be a spiritual law that we cannot do this kind of work effectively all by ourselves: we need the fellowship of others who do it with us. Why did Jesus send the apostles off two by two? Did one fill in what the other lacked? Did one pray while the other spoke? Did their fellowship sustain them when discouraged, and hold them in line when heady through success? We are not meant to lean on one another, nor to dominate one another: but we are meant to depend on one another, to learn from one another, to step up and take responsibility where we see it needed, and at all times to demonstrate the corporate aspect of the whole Christian program. Many of us first become spiritually articulate with those who have an understanding of spiritual things: thus we learn to become articulate with those who do not have such an understanding.

There is a certain point at which nothing can prevent the blooming of a flower, save cutting it from the stem on which it grows: and there is a certain point at which nothing can prevent the blossoming of a man's faith in witness, save to cut him off from Christ. We never know when we shall be met with an opportunity if only we are ready. During my summer vacation it seemed right to gather together some of my young college undergraduate neighbors on Sunday nights. The mother of one of them began it by saying, "I wish you could see something of my son." He came to the church where I was preaching, we met and made friends. I said I should like to see him sometime. "When?" was his response. "How about to-night?" A friend of his stood by, and I said, "Let us three meet, and bring along any others of your friends, and let's chew the fat about religion." When I got there, there were eight of them, ranging from about nineteen to twenty-two. Soon they were asking questions, and I was answering them mostly by stories of people and situations where faith was at work. We talked from eight till eleven thirty! We met every Sunday evening after that. Four others joined us at different times. We laughed, we talked seriously, they said exactly what they thought, I kept only a kind of thread of unity and purpose running through it all, toward the end we prayed together. Several of them have taken spiritual steps ahead, most of them have begun praying daily, several have definite "projects" in their minds, i.e., people they want to help—in many instances a member of the older generation, that bankrupt generation of mine that thought they could do without religion and have harvested such a crop of breakdown, alcoholism and divorce. One of these fellows was working for a woman who is an alcoholic. Shyly he suggested we pray for her, and we did, all together. At the meeting two weeks later, he reported that she had stopped drinking just about the time we prayed for her. "Believe it or not, that's when it was!" he says. There had been a couple of real talks with her on his part, appropriately modest as he was many years younger, but firm and honest and courageous, too. He has talked of what has happened to him, with an older man, and with two "postdeb" girl friends. He had begun to catch the wonderful contagion!

At this point of writing, a car drew up outside the study. It was the garbage-burner salesman again! "I've been awfully busy on a new deep-freeze outfit that we are getting out," he said, "but I can't get out of my head some of the things you said when I was here before." He had been back to Alcoholics Anonymous, and been to church, and he had been saying his prayers again. With his family away on vacation, the last weekend was full of temptation to drink again: but he had prayed and warded it off. The whole idea of faith in Christ was growing on him. I asked him if he thought the time had come for an unreserved decision for Christ in his life, and he said he thought it had. We went over item by item just what it meant. He knew he must turn over to God his anxiousness about his business and the support of his family, the pulls of selfishness, of drink, and of lust, and he must let God direct him about the making and spending of money. Together we made that decision in prayer. He went off fortified with (1) a daily plan for keeping up his devotional and prayer life, (2) the names of three books he was going to buy to get started, including *Abundant Living* and *Faith That Works*, (3) a plan for family devotions when his wife and children get home, (4) a plan to conduct his business so that all who work for him may at the same time find an experience of Christ, and (5) the names of two men to whom he was going as soon as possible, with the aim of helping them if he could. He wants, he says, to get off the receiving end now, and begin getting on the giving end of religion. As he left, I recalled to him Chesterton's great saying about the Franciscans, "They saw to it that anyone who met one of them by chance should have a spiritual adventure."

But why, *why* is it so much more possible to set alight and afire some of these who are not far from paganism than it is to set the church people afire? Have they been hopelessly burned over? Have they heard the words so long that all the music has gone out of them? Have the sharp points of the Gospel been worn down for them like the teeth of an old file? Why is there so little evidence, in our invisible souls, or on the outside, of a "before" and "after"? One of God's fiery spokesmen says, "If you can get religion without knowing it, you can lose it without missing it." Is that it? Sometimes as one seeks to rouse the lethargic folk that occupy the places of Christians in the church, it is to find them immune to ignition —as if instead of being like excelsior with which to light the fire, they were more like shredded asbestos! They *will* not take fire! It makes one think of the trenchant words of George Macdonald, "As for any influence from the public offices of religion, a contented soul may glide through them all for a long life, unstruck to the last, buoyant and evasive as a bee among hail-stones."

And yet—it can and does come to us sometimes with great power—as witness some of the stories found earlier in this book, where a long-standing church deadness has been raised to life again. But it must come to more people and much more quickly. We cannot afford the luxury of waiting till we "feel" like it, or till we have let somebody sweat and labor over us a little longer. The time is short . . .

Arnold J. Toynbee, in his *A Study of History*, says that of the twenty-six civilizations known to history, sixteen are dead and buried, two of the other ten are in their last agonies, and seven of the final eight are under threat of annihilation by the eighth, which is our own Western civilization. "Of the living civilizations everyone has already broken down and is in process of disintegration except our own." But all is not well with our own, which may go the way of all the rest unless some new and creative factor comes into play. "We are not compelled," he says, "to submit the riddle of our fate to the blind arbitrament of statistics. The divine spark of creative power is still alive in us, and, if we have the grace to kindle it into flame, then the stars in their courses cannot defeat our efforts to attain the goal of human endeavour."

Mankind is epitomized today in Christian, of Bunyan's immortal *Pilgrim's Progress.* Upon a wide scale our contemporaries wait to meet one who will do for them what Evangelist did for Christian. Let us close with this ageless story.

When Pilgrim has learned from his Book that he is in the City of Destruction, he is troubled by night and day. One day while walking in the fields he is reading, and "greatly distressed in his mind," saying, "What shall I do to be saved?" Then he looks "this way and that way, as if he would run; yet he stood still, because, as I perceived, he could not tell which way to go. I looked then, and saw a man named Evangelist coming to him, who asked, 'Wherefore dost thou cry?' He answered, 'Sir, I perceive by the Book in my hand, that I am condemned to die, and after that to come to judgment; and I find that I am not willing to do the first, nor able to do the second. . . . Then said Evangelist, 'If this be thy condition, why standest thou still?' He answered, 'Because I know not whither to go.' Then he gave him a parchment roll, and there was written within, 'Flee from the wrath to come.' The man, therefore, read it, and looking upon Evangelist very carefully, said, 'Whither must I fly?' Then said Evangelist, pointing with his finger over a very wide field, 'Do you see yonder wicket gate?' The man said, 'No.' Then said the other, 'Do you see yonder shining light?' He said, 'I think I do.' Then said Evangelist, 'Keep that light in your eye, and go directly thereto, so shalt thou see the gate; at which, when thou knockest, it shall be told thee what thou shalt do.' So I saw in my dream that the man began to run. Now, he had not run far from his own door, but his wife and children perceiving it, began to cry after him to return; but the man put his fingers in his ears, and ran on, crying, 'Life! life! Eternal life.' So he looked not behind him, but fled towards the middle of the plain."